Flowers
And
High Heels

A Modern Day
High School Love Story

Written by Stephen Brown

DEDICATION

For anyone and everyone who has experienced hurt from the world and for the girl with the white Audi. I love you.

CONTENTS

PROTECT STEPHEN BROWN

A LETTER FROM THE AUTHOR

As I wrote this novel, I struggled with the best way to begin the story. My first idea was to just dive right in, but after much thought, I've decided to give you this letter as a ticket for your ride. If you'd rather jump right in, I understand and will not discourage you from doing that. If you would like a guide in understanding this embodiment of art, you should keep reading.

Death. Inevitable for everyone reading; inevitable for the characters that you and I play every day of our lives. From Lucas Sterling to Tim Tylers, you will see a piece of yourself in this. On every page. The subject of this novel was, at first, a high school relationship gone downhill, but as I wrote and wrote and wrote, it became something much bigger than Stephen Brown and his own personal woes. The goal was to create a story that you could read and feel less alone with, and to make something that would create a new world for me. But things spiraled. The goal for rolling this out was to create an experience. I wanted you to live this story as you read it.

Knowing that I had to sacrifice personal grievances I intended to tackle in order to reflect the real environment that you and I walk into every Monday through Friday, I chose to change roles and watch high school as an outsider. I kept myself at a distance for months, watching the way my peers acted. I listened to my friends talk about topics from their drug habits to their home lives. I watched the way kids teared up when they brought up their real life problems. I tried to help as best I could, but I could not sacrifice the ultimate goal – to create a relatable piece of art and a guide for kids who are struggling so they can finally feel like there is hope in their lives.

Everyone has to cope at some point in their lives. Some people may use religion, some may use music, some may use art, and some may just express their feelings directly. I realized that kids do not generally turn to literature as a way of coping. Maybe it's the technology the world has begun to turn to for everything, or maybe it's the fact that kids have embedded in their heads the thought that books are boring. I struggled with this. I knew I wanted to save someone's life when I saw the outreach and effect that a poem I'd written, performed and released a video of had on people. I knew I wanted to do this act through literature, even after I released a struggling collection of my writings from 2016 and came to the realization that kids don't read anymore. I was conflicted, to say the least, but I had a sliver of hope left when I opened up a Google document and began the first draft of Chapter 1.

Some people will take the narrative of young Lucas Sterling and relate it to me. I knew this when I announced the novel on social media. My plea to those people is this:

If you pick this novel up knowing that Stephen Brown wrote it, and you hold any expectation because of that, you will not understand or even fathom the extent that the words I've written are meant to travel. I ask you – please – to get rid of every preconceived notion and just read. Read and read and read and read. Analyze if you'd like; annotate if you want to make your teachers proud. The important point I'm trying to make here is: Let Lucas Sterling be you. Let Emma Illiano be you. Let Tim Tylers and James Joshua be you.

Do not walk into this expecting Lucas Sterling to be the embodiment of Stephen Brown and try to piece my life together. That is not why I wrote this and that is not why I fought to give this novel away for free, unfiltered and uncensored. I need you to know that Stephen Brown is not Lucas Sterling. Nobody is Lucas Sterling. But Lucas Sterling is everybody.

If you take this into account in reading this, you will live through the experience of Flowers and High Heels. If not, then you will be living through an experience that you chose to run from.

Thank you for reading my novel. Thank you for sharing this experience with me.

I love you. Be good. Don't die.
And drink water.

– S. Brown

PROTECT STEPHEN BROWN

PROLOGUE

Morning. A man wakes to the ringing of the phone in his hotel room. It's the front desk, his scheduled wake up call. He gets up, goes to the bathroom and turns on the shower. The TV is still on from last night. Fox News. Typical. He's only in the city for business; he hates the city. He gets into the shower, and feels the hot water burn his skin, just the way he likes. After getting out, he pulls a freshly dry-cleaned suit from the closet.

He listens to the woman reporting the morning news.

"As the 2016 presidential race comes to the end ..." the man begins to tune her voice out. He is tired of hearing about politics.

He lays his suit jacket across the bed in his room, and goes into the bathroom to brush his teeth. Toothpaste drips onto the collar of his shirt. The man curses under his breath. He isn't supposed to care; he's the boss anyway. He could practically show up in an Adidas tracksuit and still be given the utmost attention. He just cared about his appearance a little too much – something his son taught him.

The man walks out of the bathroom to check his messages. He stops when the woman reporting the news says a name that he knows.

"...the boy's name is Lucas Sterling. Last night, he live streamed his suicide attempt, and is now on life support. In the stream, done through Twitter, he exposed the people who'd led him to this point before taking a leap into his neighborhood pool with weights attached to his ankles. We express our well wishes to Lucas and his family in this time, as do many Twitter users. His name has been mentioned over 127 thousand times in the past 9 hours since his stream started."

A picture of the boy, who can't be older than 16, pops onto the television; he bears a striking resemblance to the man watching.

The man quickly turns to his phone. He had 65 missed texts and 115 missed calls.

Most from his wife, his family and his close friends.

He listens to the voicemail his wife left him. He can hear her crying.

"Lucas is on life support. He went all the way this time. He tried to drown himself. Get back to town, now."

The man throws his phone across the room before running to the safe in his closet. He grabs his wallet, his watch and a wad of $100 bills before grabbing his bags and leaving the hotel room. He rushes down to the lobby and out onto the street. He calls his wife as soon as he is outside.

"I just saw it on the news and then I saw all of your texts and calls. I'm on my way. I love you. Tell him I love him."

The man hails a cab. As soon as he gets inside, the tears begin to fall. The **rose** bushes in the city are at full bloom. They're all **pink**.

THE MOVIE I WAS WATCHING

As best as I can remember, this is how it happened. I fell in love with Emma Illiano on the 29th day of August, 2015. Coincidentally, this happened to be the same day that I broke up with Kelly Wilson, a 16-year-old caring, and insanely spontaneous, punk pop girl who did not deserve the heartbreak that I'd just brought upon her.

Emma and I crossed paths thanks to two mutual friends who were currently dating – my best friend, Kyle McDonald, and Emma's close friend, Jewel LaCresse. I had known of Emma's existence long before the fateful day in August, thanks to an open mic night earlier in the summer that resulted in Jewel and Kyle meeting.

I had been at the open mic night with the intention of performing a song I'd written, but I backed out at the last minute due to the prolonged disease that I had suffered from birth, *throwing away every chance I get at a happy ending.* You may or may not have heard of it. Kyle and I had gone to the open mic together, and I pointed Jewel out to him when I saw she was with all the rich girls from Somberton High School (Somby for short).

Kyle had been there for me because … wait. I am so sorry; you haven't even had the chance to meet me or figure out what I'm doing. My name is Lucas Blaise Sterling, and I am 15 years old. I'm in a pretty weird position right now so I figured I'd let you share this experience of reflection with me. You'll understand later.

Anyway, Kyle was there to show support for me, because he was about to be a senior and he could put me on to all the upperclassmen at the monthly open mic. He'd also been my best friend for going on nine years. So, after me backing out of performing, he convinced me to walk up to the girls and start talking to them. He said it was the only way I could redeem myself.

I wasn't attracted to any of the girls because they seemed to care too much about what people thought (hypocritical of me, I know), but I did want to meet some new people considering the fact that, at the time, everyone from my old school had given up on me. I admit it was Kyle who asked them who was going to be transferring to his school (my old one), Drivestone High, due to the overcrowding at Somby.

I remember Jewel listing off a bunch of kids I didn't know or care to know, and then she finished off with the name "Emma Illiano."

"Emma..." I repeated. (Side note: I have no idea why this name struck out to me more than the others.) "I like that name."

Now, that's the backstory. Here is how I came to fall in love with Emma Illiano.

I was never a big fan of "sliding" into girls DMs (direct messages). Many guys would have done that in 2015 because they didn't think it was corny, but I can say I was ahead of my time with that one (haha). It tended to be high school boys who dressed like they were in fraternities who did that type of stuff, and me being a scrawny, freshman boy who wears tight jeans and was going to an art school, I'd have looked stupid. I also despised pink shorts and button downs that were too big for me – classic frat boy attire. Girls were really interested in that at that point because, like I said, they didn't realize how corny it was.

So, moving on, after crafting a long plan – with the help of Kyle and Jewel – for how to go about speaking to Emma without performing a "slide," I commented under one of Emma's *only* Instagram pictures asking for her to text me if she wanted. Emma had two photos of herself alone on social media; the rest were pictures with her friends. This fact, tied together with me not being on my anxiety medication, made me begin to wonder if Emma was shy and that I had come off too strong. I immediately regretted my move and feared I looked stupid.

My fears were quickly silenced when Emma responded, less than five minutes later.

The comment said: "Hey, text me!" and was followed by a DM from her containing a New Jersey phone number.

I'll be honest and tell you that I was skeptical at first, thinking that Emma may have given me a fake number to let me down easily. This thought was also put to rest after I shot Emma a text asking if it was indeed Emma Illiano and was given confirmation. I took a screenshot of the convo and sent it to my group chat with Kyle and Jewel, with a text saying, "I did that" and the smirking emoji. I **smirked** a lot, so that was usually my top emoji on the list.

Anyways, on this night, the 29th of August, I talked to the infamous Emma Illiano, the most visually attractive creature in the small world I had experienced in my near 15 years. This is the first instance that turned my pride up to a new level. It stayed on that level for near a year.

I was *not* a big fan of video chatting, but that night I (impulsively) asked Emma to FaceTime because I wanted to hear her voice and see if she was real or if I was stuck inside of a dream. She accepted the request, and that night we talked for hours on. When she answered the FT call, her long dark hair was down, falling in a cascade around her shoulders. She wore no makeup and was dressed in an oversized **pink** t-shirt, which looked very comfortable. I was mesmerized by Emma's lack of concern about how people thought she looked; it was so different to me from how most Somby girls acted. Later on, I'd tell people that I didn't fall in love with Emma until I saw her in person, but secretly, deep down, I fell in love with her that night when I saw every inch of her beauty.

Emma had beautiful teeth, and her skin was so clear that I didn't even realize that she wasn't wearing makeup until she apologized for her "bum" appearance. We chatted that night for three hours, never having a dull moment. We both liked the fact that it was possible to be transparent with each other and not feel any judgment.

"You're actually a really sweet boy," she told me. "The fact that you try to help people with their problems is a gift, something I like."

My illness that had appeared at the open mic decided to make a reappearance that night when I decided against telling Emma how happy I was to be able to finally talk to her after the months between that night and when I'd first heard her name. Instead, I talked to her about the breakup with Kelly, because I didn't feel necessarily happy with how I'd handled things. I knew I had done the right thing, but it hurt knowing that I was the cause of someone else's pain.

In all honesty, I had broken up with Kelly Wilson because she wanted me to put an end to her virginity. Unfortunately, I was not in love with Kelly like I'd pretended to be (bad habit), so I could not perform such a socially constructed "important" act. This decision would come to define much more in my life than I could have imagined. I don't regret what I did; I regret making as big of a deal of it as I did.

Emma made me feel happy, that night of the 29th. She told me that I was a good person for doing what I did with the Kelly situation and that she was sure Kelly would understand one day. (Spoiler: Kelly now loves me and we are bffs.)

Emma and I had just started high school days before we met. We both happened to be going into schools with a majority of people we didn't know – of course, this was unintentional on Emma's part. As I mentioned earlier, Somby had become overpopulated so Emma and hundreds of other kids were redistributed to different schools in the district. She wound up at Drivestone High.

I was the one to end the conversation on that late night, with a request to talk to Emma the next day. She accepted with no doubt suggested in her tone. I went to bed and didn't have a nightmare at all. I even woke up happy the next day, ready for school.

I was a smart boy on paper back then, I suppose. I got good grades, kept my head down, and made witty comments in my head, rather than vocalizing them. The only "dumb" part of me was my habit of smoking cigarettes. I was a big, big fan of **Newports** straight out of middle school. Emma was also very intelligent; she was ranked with the 14th highest GPA in the freshman class at Drivestone (not as impressive as you think, considering half of Drivestone also thought that the Confederate flag was still a national flag in 2015).

"Lucas, you're a genius. The world has needed someone like you for years," Emma would come to tell me later on in our relationship, when I told her that I wasn't really smart – I just knew how to talk. "You give me hope for the future of our generation."

The next day, the last day of August, a Monday, I got out of school and immediately texted Emma asking what time I could call. She said it'd be a few hours, but she promised to call me as soon as her cheerleading practice ended and she was home. I decided I'd fill the afterschool hours, while Emma was at practice, hanging out with Kyle and one of our close friends, Matt, making sure to warn them that I'd have to duck out as soon as Emma was able to talk. I sat outside that day with my friends, taking pictures of the blue, cloudless sky with my iPhone while discussing how much stress came with school.

"My point is, 80 percent of the stuff they teach you in school is irrelevant in your day-to-day life," I announced as I lit up a **cigarette.** "We're either going to end up unemployed with no hope and in inevitable poverty or employed in a specific field where so many topics in school will just exit our brains."

Matt responded with annoyance in his voice.

"Dude, it's not that deep. Everyone has got to make money and school is what gets us there… It sucks but that's how it is; we just have to deal with it."

"But, like, isn't that stupid?" I egged on. I had a habit of doing this to people like Matt, who wanted to be regular.

"Why should I spend 80 years of my life 'dealing' when I could be making a change?" I asked.

Matt and Kyle looked down at the ground, shaking their heads hopelessly. I stopped snapping photos and looked up at the sky.

"Haven't you ever thought about this world and what we're doing in it? Most of our jobs are outsourced to different countries, human beings have to become slaves to financial aid for a good job, and our parents expect us to go to the college they want and follow through with a specific major," I chuckled. "And we have the audacity to speak about sports or elections being rigged, when we have rigged our own lives."

"Bro, take it easy. The world could end tomorrow and none of that would matter. Stop tripping so hard," Kyle shot back.

"Yes, that's true. But, any of our individual lives could end tomorrow! Why would you want to die being regular? Who programmed it into your brain that your life won't be worth anything once you are dead?" I asked.

I could be very persistent when it came to a topic I felt strongly about. I'd collect my thoughts over time, and if I didn't have enough info or background knowledge on an important topic, I wouldn't speak on it until I did.

I looked down at my phone and saw that Emma had texted me. She was on her way home from cheer practice. I put my cigarette out and began to clean up the cans of Cherry Vanilla Coca-Cola I'd been drinking.

"Whatever," I said impatiently, trying to hide my excitement about my next statement.

"Emma is about to be home anyway, so I'll catch you guys tomorrow!" I said with a smile.

Before Kyle and Matt had finished their goodbyes, I was in the house and halfway up the stairs. Just as I tapped the FaceTime icon on my phone, Mom yelled up to tell me it was time for dinner. I quickly texted Emma to say I needed 10 minutes before I could talk.

"That's fine," she responded. "I'm going to take a shower."

I smiled, then ran downstairs where, as is the custom, I blessed the food for my family with my quick, 10-word blessing, "Thank you, God, for this meal. Please send us blessings."

"What's got you so excited?" Mom asked me quite politely.

"Oh, nothing. I just want to finish watching a movie. How was you guys' day?" I motioned this time to both my mother and my father, who seemed to be completely wrapped up in his food.

"Not too bad – boring like usual. How are you liking the new school?" Dad asked with his mouth full.

"It's fine … not too exciting," I responded, "My history teacher is cool though. He used to be a cop so he's a bit uptight and intimidating, but he makes us think and I like that."

"That's nice," Mom quietly stated while looking down at her plate, deciding whether she wanted to eat more. "How's theater going?"

I was at my new school, Leigh Academy of Arts (LAA for short), for the theater program there. It was a nationally renowned high school theater program with the best director in the southeast, Jerry Thomason, at the head of it. Kids who went to LAA for theater almost always got accepted into major colleges and went on to do major shows around the globe. I'd gotten the lead role in my 8th grade play, *Aladdin*, and when I auditioned for LAA, I was immediately taken under Thomason's wing because he had seen me in the show when he was scouting for talent.

"We're still in orientation right now, though Mr. Thomason is amazing. I feel like I didn't even know how to act before I set foot in that classroom. He teaches you something new every day that seems so simple but can make or break a performance," I answer, trying not to show too much emotion. I wasn't good at being "passionate" about things because I was used to being judged by those around me for it. For instance, if I were to say that music saved my life, I would be burned and questioned.

Our family dinner was finished in eight minutes, which gave me more time to do something to my hair and practice smiling.

I washed my plate off and darted back up the stairs, yelling, "Thank you for dinner!" along the way. Once I got up to my room, I grabbed my phone and saw a text from Emma saying that she's ready to talk. So much for cleaning up. I called her and waited for the video chat to load. The minute I saw Emma's face, I realized that my parents couldn't possibly understand the importance of the movie I was watching.

A PRETTY LUCKY KID

At this point in my life, I was a pretty lucky kid. Girls weren't all about me like I wished they were, but it didn't bug me. I was a privileged, suburban white male who didn't have to worry about anything except getting accepted into the college I wanted to attend. Somehow, my narcissism really took a turn for the worse along the way and I found reasons to be sad. It's almost as if I rejected the privilege I'd been given because I was addicted to the depression that had been genetically passed down to me.

The more comfortable Emma got with me, the more beautiful she became. I, on the other hand, was really awkward, sad and quirky most of the time. Emma thought I was cute because of these attributes, but I thought that opinion would change once she met me and saw how I literally walked with no purpose in my step.

I met Emma in person for the first time on the 3rd day of September. I had decided to attend one of the Drivestone JV football games where she was cheering. I was a closet football fan. I loved watching it and watching people get excited and happy over it. That night though, the only thing I could focus on was Emma. Her charisma and attitude were attributes that I would come to owe my life to. She was so beautiful, even when she was yelling and sweating and chanting cliché cheers.

I hugged Emma the minute she came off the field at halftime. I told her she looked really cute in her cheer outfit, and that she was "doing good out there." I didn't really know how one would cheer badly but I suppose a compliment is a compliment. She did look amazing, and I don't know if that was due to beauty or skill. But it had me mesmerized.

"I'm sorry that I'm a sweaty mess. I know this is probably unattractive for our first time meeting," Emma said.

"Don't apologize," I responded with a **smirk** that turned into a warm smile. "The first night we ever spoke, you had no makeup on and your hair was down and nothing had been done to it, and I still thought you looked astonishing."

I wasn't used to smiling so much until I started talking to Emma. Whatever it was that had developed between us felt like a dream, and I was falling hopelessly in love with her. Love was a weird thing; I ever so helplessly became the most vulnerable I'd ever been and still had a warm heart. It scared me, but it made me feel like the world was so beautiful. Love contradicted itself as much as I did. Maybe that's why I latched onto it.

That night was a Thursday. After the game, I took a picture with Emma. She made me promise not to post it because she thought she looked "greasy."

It was Saturday, September 5, 2015, around 7 p.m., when I professed my feelings to Emma Illiano. We had just finished getting dinner at Joe's.

"I just think you're really gorgeous, and you make me feel like Heaven exists ... and I like that feeling," I spilled. "You are kind to me and you know how to keep me at bay. I can't compare it to anything because nothing else has ever made me feel this way, but I know it is something special."

"Lucas, you're a sweet boy, I really mean it…" Emma began, "but, I'm sort of talking

19

to a boy right now. I like you but I don't want this to be a competition for you. I do care and I want to be with you, but I also want to be with him."

Stunned, but determined not to show it, I responded with my head down.

"I understand."

Truthfully, I'll never understand why Emma turned me down that evening. Like I said, I was a good kid. Honestly. I didn't try to have sex with Emma or even get naked pictures from her. I decided I'd not let her see that I was upset because I didn't want her to feel bad. I knew I'd treat her better than anyone else would, but I had to accept that that might not happen.

I was out of my mind for thinking Emma Illiano would ever fall in love with a boy like me.

I had a nightmare that night and awoke sweating profusely and feeling insanely dehydrated. In the dream, I watched Emma slowly push me away to be with the other boy she was talking to. It was this nightmare that caused me to make a decision I would come to regret. I was done with letting the "illness" I'd spoken about earlier destroy my life. I stayed up for the rest of the night, chain smoking **cigarettes** on the roof of my house, trying to figure out what I was to do about everything that had happened. I had nothing going for me except for the fact that I had a way with words and I knew my way around the Internet.

I've always been braver over the Internet. I wasn't on Auernheimer's level, but I was close. I liked to challenge everything people thought – even the things I believed in. I wanted reasoning for everything. I thought that made kids smarter. And I believed we all needed to be a little smarter.

Emma didn't want me to tell anyone we were even speaking. She was afraid of what people would say, and I could not blame her. She was Emma Illiano and I was Lucas Sterling. She reminded me of that from day 1, and I never understood that it wasn't a compliment until later.

One evening in September, Mom, Dad and I took the trek to a town a couple hours south of ours to visit with my sister and brother-in-law. I texted with Emma the whole way there and we had no dull moments. It was just a day trip, so I wasn't too upset about having to go. I was actually very excited about the trip.

But once there, I got very bored sitting around and talking to my family. I snuck away and called Emma. I'd taken a lot of time that day to think things out and decided that I was going to tell Emma that I was in love with her. I chose to do this because I refused to let our **cigarette** burn with no drag. So, I walked to a field, laid down in the grass on a blanket, and FaceTimed her.

"I'm falling in love with you and I don't *want* to stop. I want you to choose me because nobody will ever make you as happy as I can. This might ruin everything, but I can't contain my feelings anymore and I don't want to play games. I am falling in love with you, Emma Illiano, and I want the chance to make you fall in love with me."

As soon as the words were out of my mouth, I regretted them. Who was I to tell Emma what she should do?

"Oh, shit," was all that Emma could muster up in response.

This was not a good sign. She didn't expect this. She thought I was done with that dream. I had to backtrack.

"I'm sorry. I'm going to go. I should never have let myself become so vulnerable. Please don't hate …" I began, before Emma cut me off.

"Lucas Sterling, don't you dare apologize for being the sweetest boy on the planet," she said. "You're a blessing to this world, and I want to be with you."

I was wary of this, thinking she may not mean what she was saying.

"Don't tell me that just because you feel bad that I like you and you want to shield my heart," I started off slowly, choosing my words carefully, "I am all about you and I *will* change your life if you will just give me the chance."

"I'm not lying to you or shielding you from anything," she responded with the signature smile that still takes my breath away. "I like you, Lucas Sterling. I think you're cute and thoughtful, and I want to be the girl to give you what you deserve."

This had to be a dream. I woke up every day for months praying that it wasn't.

Emma and I began hanging out every weekend. I went to every one of her games, and every time, I'd sit right in front of where she cheered so I could distract her with my **smirks**. This time in our relationship was impossible to explain at that point in our lives. But now, having grown, I appreciate words enough to talk about it and admit that this was the moment in time that inspired me to write. Words were always synonymous with melodrama until I met Emma and realized words were all I had going for me.

In mid-September, while on FaceTime after just getting home from a dinner date, we decided to make "us" official. Emma and I started posting pictures together and we became 100 percent exclusive with each other. We never really decided on a date, but we chose to celebrate our "anniversary" on the third day of September. We chose that day because it was the first day we met in person, at the game.

That night, before the FaceTime, on our date, Emma wore **high heels** and I brought her two **pink roses**. One of the roses was artificial, and it signified my love for her – never dying.

Being in a relationship and not going to school with the person wasn't as bad as everyone acted like it was. LAA was a good school for me to attend. It was full of high school kids who liked art and were mostly Democrats, except for a few outcasts. Mr. Thomason was the best teacher I'd ever had. An aged, cranky wise man, he knew more about acting than half of the directors in Hollywood. I'd like to put on the record, so there are no misconceptions, that Emma gave me the passion to create. But Mr. Thomason taught me how to use it.

Emma wasn't a big fan of Drivestone but, then again, who was? It was full of Republican, Confederate-flag waving, country kids who didn't care about anything and simply regurgitated their parents' opinions.

To this day, I still cannot remember the moment that Emma confessed her love for me, but I do like to imagine. Sometimes I think it was on a night that we cuddled together and listened to music, like in my good dreams. In reality, it was probably over a text message or while she was high, but imagination never hurts.

The relationship that Emma and I shared was unlike anything either of us had expected to find. We were both intelligent and well rounded. In my artistry, I was a little of a hometown legend. I pushed limits and did things nobody wanted to understand. Emma was the most beautiful human being I had ever laid eyes on. That was reaffirmed every day for many months. Kids at LAA compared us to Kimye a lot, and I loved it because that's how I wanted people to view us.

I had been a writer for many years, and a reader, but I had never had the courage to share my writings with the world until I met

Emma and saw that beauty was real. I started releasing my writings online in December, to my small 400 follower count, and it boosted my clout (slang for reputation). Everyone who read my works said they loved what I said because I wrote just like I acted – different from what anyone in my town had seen. I believe that this time in my life sparked my pretentious attitude that I still possess to this day. Girls began to notice me a little more, and everywhere I went, someone seemed to compliment my writing. My newfound popularity did not make my relationship with Emma any easier, and we fought constantly.

"Guys want to have sex with you. All I hear is 'Ah bro, you have to hit that,' but I don't even try because I respect you. You don't even curve guys anymore, you just think that you can be friends with people who only want you for your body and that I'm supposed to be cool with it." I remarked.

"I just don't understand why you have to think that since everyone wants to have sex with me, I'm doing it," Emma said chillingly.

"That's not what I'm saying, babe. I'm saying it just bugs me how you don't shut people down when they talk to you like that. *Do you* want them?" I asked with genuine curiosity.

"No, Lucas. I want *you*. I'm with you. We are together for a reason. I'm in love with you," Emma proclaimed, this time with a nicer tone.

I retreated.

"Okay, I'm sorry. I'll leave it all alone. I'm sorry."

"It's fine," Emma said, obviously meaning it *wasn't* fine.

I surrendered. As usual.

"I'm going to just go to sleep because you're hurting my feelings. Goodnight. I love you."

"Okay, whatever. I love you, too," responded Emma coldly.

That night, I had another nightmare. Waking up crying and in a pool of sweat and vomit is definitely on my top 10 list of things that make me sad as hell. I had dreamt about Emma cheating on me with another guy, and it made me feel nauseous. The only thing that could calm me down was Emma's voice, and I knew that, so I called her. She answered after five rings.

"Hello, Lucas? What'd you do?" Emma asked, obviously irritated and suspecting something.

"Nothing. I had a nightmare about – nothing, that isn't important. I wanted to talk to you because you make me feel okay," I said trying to sonically make her picture the hopeless smile in my voice. I always loved being extremely nice in return to what I thought was someone's attempt to hurt my feelings. Emma's rude answer was an attempt to hurt my feelings, in my honest opinion.

"Oh, okay. I'm sorry, baby. What was it about?" Emma asked softly. She immediately felt guilt for how she had answered the phone, I could tell by her change of tone.

I panicked. I didn't want to upset Emma or reveal my irrational thoughts, so I lied.

"Uh, I can't remember. I just know I woke up crying and you were all I could think about," I said in an unsure tone.

That seemed to work.

"I love you, baby," she said. "Try to sleep if you can. Call me if you can't."

"Okay, I'll try. I love you, beautiful. I'm sorry about today," I said with a somewhat sad voice.

"Don't worry about any of that," Emma said tenderly. "Just try to sleep. I love you. Goodnight."

PINK ROSES

After this incident, anger became the fuel in my relationship with Emma. We, consistently, fought twice a week. The worst arguments always stemmed from jealousy. I did not like hearing about other guys, and Emma did not like hearing about other girls. Eventually, the fighting got to a point that was unbearable. I brought this up over a phone call one night after we'd had a rough day.

"What are you suggesting?" Emma asked after I said that we couldn't keep fighting like we had been, sounding hurt.

"I'm just suggesting that we both start to make an effort, or we should start to reassess our relationship," I responded calmly.

I've typically always been the rational individual in every relationship I'd been in. Even with Emma, I started off being rational.

I didn't like fighting. I was petty and sometimes I came across as rude, but I refused to let those two miniscule attributes in that time of my life determine how people viewed me.

"So you're suggesting that we break up if we continue to fight?" Emma asked sternly.

"We are only a month into being exclusive and this is already happening too much," I replied with an irritable bit of sass.

Emma knew I had a point, but she wouldn't dare admit that to me. No ordinary couple was supposed to act the way we did so early in a relationship. Then again, we were no *ordinary* couple.

After this particular argument, our relationship began to run steady. Emma and I stopped fighting so much and started seeing each other a lot more. I started smoking a lot more than I had previously to keep my anxiety from killing me. I wasn't really big on drugs but cigarettes made me feel a little less ... heavy, I suppose.

Emma and I participated in no sexual acts for the first month of our relationship. We'd occasionally feel each other up through our clothes while making out, but I wouldn't dare be the person to cut the sexual tension between us. (My illness ruined a lot of cool chances I'd had at "getting some.") My sexual thoughts were always neutral when it came down to it, and I tried to keep them that way. I held possession of my own body, and it was my duty to care about others'.

This changed when Lilly Printo set foot in my broadcasting class. Lilly was one member of the largest senior class LAA had ever seen. She was assigned as the peer tutor for our class, mainly because it was easy for her to get an A in tutoring, and it was her senior year so she was ready to have one class she literally didn't have to do anything in. Lilly had heard of me through the wire at LAA, because she was also a writer. She reached out to me on Twitter through direct message one night.

"Lucas Sterling," was all she messaged me.

"Ms. Lilly Printo," I responded, calling her Ms. because she was technically one of my "teachers."

"You are making waves. I'd like to do some photography with you and interview you for a blog," Lilly messaged back, following with her phone number and a link to her photography Instagram and her most recent article.

Lilly Printo was a peculiar being. She was smart and witty, and she told me she saw a lot of herself in me. This was weird to me because she came into this life before me, and she's saying that she is like *me*. She was a devout feminist and she loved to make fun of Donald Trump. I admired it and I thought she would be a good ally to have.

Lilly was cool and she showed obvious romantic interest in me from the beginning, though I attempted to silence this interest only a week into our friendship. We were in class and she came up behind me and started brushing her fingers through my hair and telling me I looked hot.

"Look, you know I like Emma and am with her for a reason. It is nothing against you, but it isn't cool for us to be anything more than what we already are as friends." We were walking to the same building after class.

"Lucas, I totally get that and would never want to make you uncomfortable. You are a good guy and I hope Emma treats you how you deserve. Friends forever, right?" Lilly spoke eloquently as always.

"Of course." I smiled back.

Simple, I thought. Too simple.

It was a rainy Monday afternoon, when I received an anonymous Snapchat message from a user, "sretaehcdesopxe." The screen name on the account was "anonymous." The picture in the message was of Emma and a boy I did not recognize making out on someone's couch. It wasn't the couch at Emma's house, which was the first thing that struck me.

Now, like I said earlier, I am typically a rational guy. In this moment though, I became infuriated. I was tired of being walked on and I was ready to cut Emma out completely. I called her immediately and began going off on her for cheating.

"You ran off like a whore," I said with the voice of a crazy man, "I gave you the world. **I should've never even thought that you'd fall in love with a kid like me. This *was* too good to be true.**"

"Lucas, let's talk about this," Emma started. "I only did this because of our fighting. I thought you didn't care about me anymore. This is kind of your fault, and you shouldn't be so mad at me for doing what I did. Just please stay. You're the only one that gets me, and I refuse to let you go just because I made a small mistake."

"No. I may get you in the sense that I understand your problems and want to help you. But I do not get you in the sense of being my girlfriend. I never will. I love you. See if he can 'get' you, because he obviously wasn't a mistake when you were all over him." I said and ended the call.

I *wanted* to get out of the house. I chain smoked for two hours while thinking of how to cope. I didn't do well. I cut myself for the first time that night, and it really destroyed me. I had always been the beam who made people not want to hurt themselves, and as I looked myself in the mirror and at the dried blood on my wrist, I began to sob. It wasn't supposed to be this way. I now *needed* to get out of the house.

I decided to ask my friend Jimmy if he knew of any parties or get-togethers going on that weekend, and he found one for Friday night and sent me the address. Jimmy was a snake but he was good for moves so you kept in close contact with him.

I went to the party, which had mainly LAA people there, and I got sloppy drunk. In my near 15 years on the planet, I'd never even touched alcohol before that night. But I was tired of thinking and avoiding things. Anyway, I was in bad shape. My mother and father thought I was at Kyle's, but Kyle was on a date with Jewel. I knew they'd be ashamed if they saw me this way. This entire situation was a mess and I blamed it all on Emma.

As I was about to leave the party, Lilly snatched me out of nowhere and told me she wanted to smoke a cigarette with me. I kindly accepted, wondering how the burning taste of liquor would feel with smoke rolling over it. Lilly took me to her car and pulled out a box of **Newports** and we took turns chain smoking until Jimmy found me and said it was time to go.

"I can take him home. I haven't been drinking or done any drugs tonight and I live right by him," Lilly suggested.

I still would like to know how Lilly knew she lived near me even though she'd never been to my house that I knew of. Anyway, Jimmy was wary of this, but I wore him down until he agreed that I could hang with Lilly. We went back to her house, which actually was only a five-minute drive from where I lived.

"Where are your parents?" I asked.

"They're never here. We own two houses and usually we rent this one out, but I am living here for now," Lilly responded.
She took me to the master bedroom. I knew what was coming and I was not sure if I

wanted to go far with Lilly because I had no attraction to her other than as a good friend. I was stuck lying to myself thinking Lilly would be a better person than to take advantage of a freshman boy who she sort of tutored. She immediately came onto me.

"I can't have sex with you," I said. "I love Emma still. This wouldn't feel right and it would not be fair." She just nodded her head as if she respected my decision. She then unbuttoned my pants.

"Lilly, I do not want to do this. Please stop," I begged.

It was on this night in mid-October that Lilly Printo raped me. I was not entirely innocent, due to my drunkenness, but Lilly did not respect my request and took my virginity from me without my consent. This fact haunts me to this day.

I went to Emma's house eight days later. I brought her a **pink rose**. We talked. I forgave her for cheating and told her about what had happened to me with Lilly, hoping she'd understand. I knew I was kidding myself but I owed it to Emma to tell her the truth of what happened.

"A girl can't rape a boy," Emma said in an angry tone. "If you did it to get back at me, I understand. Just tell me the truth."

"Emma, I am not lying. Lilly took my virginity from me without my consent while I was intoxicated and she was 18 years old. I am 14. All of those are red flags for any rape case," I tried to explain without sounding hurt.

The truth is, I was hurt and still do hurt because of this conversation.

"You'd been drinking so you have no excuse," Emma shot back.

"Are you implying that this is my fault?" I asked angrily. "Tell me you were sober whenever you made out with whoever that dude was, *Angel Emma*," I said.

"Whatever, I am completely tired of all of this. Let's just move past all of this shit," Emma said.

And that is what we did. We did not speak about either situation to each other for weeks. Emma made sure to tell all of her friends that I "cheated" on her, and I made sure to keep bringing her pink roses, thinking this would make her stop lying about me. I was wrong.

Emma Illiano was ready for my demise. She initiated it.

BITE MY LIP

Sex was a topic that I hated speaking about after Lilly came along. She ruined it for me. I could never say that I lost my virginity to the girl who I loved, or even in a romantic way. I had to live with the fact that I lost it to a girl who did not care about me. Lilly stopped speaking to me after I confronted her in person on the Monday after everything had gone down.

She was not apologetic: "You liked what I gave to you. Don't be mad at me now because you were too dumb to say no. You got drunk and made the mistake of letting me get in your pants. If you try to tell people that I raped you or took advantage of you, I'll make sure there are major repercussions on your part."

Emma was technically a virgin, but she'd done literally everything else with Preston, her ex who came before me.

Emma went into detail about Preston a lot. I didn't like the feeling of *my* girlfriend still being caught up in her ex, especially all the things he did to her that were sexual, but I wasn't going to fight about it with her.

"I'm going to take you to an entirely different universe," I responded with a **smirk**, one day when she asked what I could do to her.

"Be my guest," Emma responded, **biting her lip**.

Emma and I did not have sex, but I did what I could to please her that day. It took 10 minutes. Everything sounded like poetry after we were done.

The next day, Emma texted me and told me she wanted us to have sex. I called her that night and we made a plan to do it the next Saturday at Emma's house. Emma wasn't nearly as nervous as I was. All I could think about was what would happen if I took her virginity and then she decided she didn't want to be with me anymore. I couldn't imagine how much that would hurt, and I did not want to know.

I let Emma perform oral sex on me on Friday, November 6th, 2015, the day before I was to take her virginity. Our sexual tension was passive at first, but when I began to kiss her, we both felt the sides of us that hid behind the curtains before show time. Emma begged me to take her virginity right then and there.

"Are you sure you don't want to wait until tomorrow?" I asked.

"I've never been more sure about anything in my life. I want to give you everything, Lucas," Emma spoke, trying to catch her breath.

I wanted Emma to be comfortable with everything that happened between us. I was scared that she'd feel as if I was forcing her or taking advantage of her. I asked her for consent five times before I decided to go through with it.

I took Emma Illiano's virginity that night. We entangled our entire lives in the sheets on her queen sized bed. She had beautiful **pink lipstick on and a pink, laced thong.** We traced constellations on each other's bodies with our mouths and we made the most beautiful music out of our **moans**. That night, all my writings, all my schoolwork, all the stress on my back was taken off along with my clothes. Nights like these would come to be our drug of choice, and they never give us a bad trip.

Emma hadn't given me any real trouble about the Lilly situation until *after* we had sex. She used it, like all my other past mistakes, to win an argument. This started the day after our first night of sex. I was planning to go to a party with my friends, and she called me to tell me how stupid that was.

"I just feel like you should have some faith in me. It's not like I'm going out and doing coke," I said with a nervous tone.

I knew that Emma would not take this statement the right way, but I had already said it. It was too late to backtrack.

"Faith? You've never believed in faith when you should have. Let me ask you, Lucas: Did you have faith in Lilly?" Emma blasted back, "Oh wait, I forgot you were *raped*," Emma said with sarcastic venom, followed by a vindictive laugh.

"I *was* raped by Lilly. I don't understand why you are too ignorant to acknowledge that. I will never get what she did out of my head, so you don't have to remind me," I said back. My voice cracked though, so Emma obviously knew she had hurt me and won.

"Lucas, I gave you a chance when nobody else even noticed you. You were just some kid who thought he was good at something he wasn't. Stop acting like I am the ignorant one," Emma said as if she knew everything.

I knew that when Emma was mad, her words and actions were poisonous. Everything in my past was fair game: all the girls I'd ever dated, all the stupid things I'd done, all the times I tried to kill myself. Anything was ammo for Emma. I knew she'd bring something up that would hurt me, so I told Emma I wanted to take a nap. She complied with my request.

"I love you," I said.

Emma responded with, "I know."

I decided I'd indirectly tweet about the situation instead of doing something dangerous. I wrote: "Funny how you can do everything for someone and they'll still try to hurt you." Bad decision.

Emma texted me within seconds, as if she had anticipated this.

"LOL. Funny how I can look past all of your flaws and still be disrespected."

I didn't think before responding. I was done with being hurt. I wanted to stand up for myself.

"You're a bitch and do not deserve me," I texted back.

Emma and I did not speak for 19 hours after the incident. I worked out and listened to music and worried about Emma the whole time. I decided to call her around 11 p.m. to talk things out with her. She answered on what I felt like was the last ring.

"Hello," she said into the phone.

She sounded busy. My heart rate sped up.

"Can we talk?" I asked.

"I'm out right now," Emma said, without any real color in her voice. "I'll call you later."

"Oh, okay. Who are you out with? What are you doing?" I asked curiously.

I knew the answer to what she was doing. She was out cheating on me and doing drugs. Exactly the things she'd just argued with me about earlier on.

"Leslie, Michelle and Tommy," Emma said, without a care. "We're just driving around and smoking."

I hung up the phone. Emma was with Michelle Minson, a girl who was notorious for sleeping her way up the social ladder in my town. She had just turned 14 the weekend before, and her body count was higher than her age. I was not one for slut shaming, but it did make me wonder: How could Emma talk so much about *my* body count being two and then go hang out with a girl whose count was eight times as much?

I was not trying to slut shame Michelle with this thought either. She had come to be my closest friend in dire times. But, really? Why did Emma only choose to judge and hurt me?

I honestly wasn't a fan of anybody that Emma was hanging out with, but they liked me because I was exceptionally good at working around high school politics.

I stayed up until 4 a.m. waiting for an "I got home safe" text from Emma. It never came. I called her, but received no answer. I rushed into a state of panic. Emma always answered the phone. I tried calling Michelle but her phone went straight to voicemail. Dead. I didn't have Leslie's number, but I knew someone who did. I called my friend, Abigail, who was angry with me for waking her up. She gave me Leslie's number and I thanked her and hung up. I called Leslie, and her phone was answered by Tom. This was all very sketchy to me. Nobody was answering their phone and when someone finally did, it's the wrong person?

"Hey, Lucas, where are you?" Tom asked hurriedly. "I'm going to have someone come get you. We got into an accident and they're transporting Emma to the hospital on the helicopter. I'm sorry, man. It was all my fault." The words came out as if they were a can of spray paint that was almost empty.

I went into shock immediately. Tom texted me the info of what to wait for. I then put on a jacket, crawled out of my bedroom window and scaled down the tree in front of my house. The car showed up in less than five minutes.

I got in, the windows were down, and I felt tears begin to flood my eyes.

AFTER THE INCIDENT

We arrived at the hospital in less than 15 minutes. I didn't know the guy who picked me up but I thanked him and tried to pay him. He wouldn't take any money, but he wished me the best and told me to stay safe. I rushed into the emergency room and was directed by a lady at the front desk to Emma's room. Her parents were already there and I could see that her mom had been crying. Emma appeared to be sleeping, but she was covered in bandages and had a cut on her face.

Emma's parents didn't like me for the first few months of our relationship, mainly because they didn't like anyone. They had recently lightened up and begun speaking to me with respect, once they read a few of my writings. Even parents didn't like me until I wrote, haha. I sort of appreciated that, but I still felt ultimately disrespected that nobody really cared about Lucas Sterling until Lucas Sterling did something irregular.

The first thing Emma's mom said to me was, "Did you know about this?"

"I knew she was out, but I didn't know if you guys knew or not. I'm sorry. I shouldn't have given her the benefit of the doubt in that situation," I responded.

"Don't beat yourself up," said Pete, Emma's father. "None of us could have prevented this stupidity." He finished with a glare at an unconscious Emma, then her mother.

Annie, Emma's mom, spoke: "The important thing is that we don't let anything like this happen ever again. I want you to update me with Emma's plans because she doesn't do that with me. I'll text you my number off of her phone."

I thought about telling them that she had only gone out because I'd made her mad. I decided against this thought because I didn't want them to think it was my fault. This was Emma's fault, and I held no blame. Still, that didn't stop the regret from settling in. I chain smoked **cigarettes** the entire night waiting for word on her condition.

Emma had no broken bones, but a lot of soreness and scrapes. She needed stitches on her shoulder also. She was able to leave the hospital at 4 the next afternoon.

Our relationship changed drastically after Emma's accident. I began writing more than ever, and a lot of it wasn't positive. Emma began yelling a lot more, also not positive. We didn't know what to attribute this to, but we knew what kept us together. It was sex and the idea that we were each the biggest things in our town; one of us for looks, the other for hard work and emotion. The concept that we were the Drivestone Kimye kept us wanting the relationship to work.

November 11th, 2016. It was the day *after* I was supposed to meet my musical hero, Trance the Trapper at his concert in my city. I wanted to bring Emma along so I got her a meet and greet pass for the concert.

Unfortunately, due to my luck, the entire concert and meet and greet was canceled due to a tornado watch. No rescheduled date had been announced at that point, but I was determined to meet Trance and tell him he'd saved my life. Trance had played a key role in my life up until I'd met Emma. Before that, my main source of healthy satisfaction was

Trance's music. It was the only positive music I knew and loved.

Anyway, back to what happened the day after all of this. I was very upset about missing the concert, so I went to a party. At this party, I bought two bars of a popular pill, **Xanax**, off of a kid I didn't really know that well. I left because the party sucked, and took them in the car on the way home. That was the last thing I remembered. I woke up the next morning not remembering what had happened the night before or who drove me home. Luckily, I'd captured most of the night with the camera on my phone.

I had been on my roof that night taking pictures of the moon and the stars, and praying. I took a video of me praying, asking God for Emma to break up with me so I'd be able to kill myself and stop making people sad.

I didn't take another bar of Xanax again for a while, because I was scared I'd do something crazy.

The day that I decided I'd not take another Xanax is the day Emma decided to tell me she didn't know if she loved me anymore.

"You're just so inconsiderate of what anyone thinks. You're one step away from looking like a sociopath," she spoke monotonously.

"Then leave, because I'm tired of being the person that brings you down all the time. You're inconsiderate and you make me feel like shit and you talk to a million different guys all the time. You don't need me like I need you," I shot back.

This was true, so I did not regret saying it. I did regret the *way* I said it though.

"Look, I was just angry. I love you and can't lose you, I just feel like you don't feel the same way," I admitted in distress.

"Maybe if you'd just come to Drivestone with me and we can have classes together and see each other everyday, things would work. If you don't want to, I understand, but I don't want to be together because I feel like I'd be happier if I was with someone who I saw everyday," Emma continued.

"Then I will come back. It's going to be hard, but I will find a way," I said.

I had therapy the day after this argument. I decided to tell my therapist that I was "contemplating suicide." I told him that if I didn't get away from LAA, I wasn't sure if I'd make good decisions. This made my therapist and parents panic and then campaign for me to be able to leave LAA at the end of the first semester.

LAA had a rule for all freshman that it was mandatory they stay at LAA for at least a full year before they transfer, but I intended to bend that rule with a doctor's order. My psychiatrist, Mrs. Jin, wrote the school a lengthy letter and, with the help of the assistant principal (who knew my family), I was granted a transfer to Drivestone for the second semester of high school, only two days after I'd requested one. I called Emma as soon as I received the news.

"The transfer was granted. I will be starting back at Drivestone on January 21st." I said it with a small tone of bitterness, and a **smirk** because I knew Emma wasn't expecting it to happen.

"I love you…" was all that Emma was able to say. She was stunned.

The problem I had with this switch was that I was actually successful at LAA. Mr. Thomason considered me one of the best actors in his class, and definitely the best writer. I knew at LAA I'd be granted a scholarship for college if I kept my grades up, but in an irrational fit of decision-making, I chose the girl over the opportunity. Though not apparent at the time, this mistake would become a key part of my future demise.

I slipped into a pit of depression after finding out I was leaving LAA. Trance hadn't announced a date for the makeup show, and I was growing anxious. I wasn't ready to transfer back to Drivestone because I'd left on shaky terms with most of my old "friends" (you'll understand later). Everyone had completely cut me out of their lives after I left Drivestone for LAA; it was taken as a personal act of treason by most. I could not vocally blame Emma for the anxiety I had, but that didn't stop me from thinking that in my head. I was angry and upset, and I had no excuse for it.

Emma also wasn't doing so well. She slipped back into her old habits of hanging out with people she didn't really know in exchange for drugs and alcohol and God knows what else.

"I hate you," I proclaimed over a phone call after Emma had been out and not returned any of my texts from 8 p.m. until 5:30 a.m.

"Hahaha," Emma started on a drunken rant. "You wish you could hate me. You know that nothing you say after 2 a.m. is legitimate. Lucas, if it wasn't for me you would've killed yourself and nobody would've cared. Now, when you kill yourself, people will care because you are my boyfriend."

"No, I genuinely didn't know how to hate until tonight," I said coldly. I was trying to keep my composure.

"Then leave," Emma shot back.

That was our signature line.

"No, because I love you also," I replied.

As complicated as this sounds, it was the truth.

I loved this person with every inch of my skin and, coincidentally, my skin ended up the most scarred from this.

"Lucas, stop trying so hard. You aren't shit at all and this little writing thing you think you have going on isn't going to get us anywhere. If I were you, I'd just focus on us and school," Emma said.

Emma always knew how to come at my weak spots when I least expected it. This cheap shot was one that particularly hurt because I had just begun taking writing seriously, with blogs reaching out to me, and my own girlfriend had already tossed it to the street. I was not happy with the outcome of this conversation so I decided to drink it away.

It was this night, in mid-November that I realized I'd have to kill myself to be happy.

I began planning. I either wanted to hang myself, overdose or drown myself. I began writing the album that I'd planned to release before I went through with one of these options. It was titled, "The End," and it was to be 10 songs, 2 skits, and one interlude long. Essentially, this album was going to be a rap album, but I began experimenting with all types of sound and decided I wanted to do something crazy. It was a lot of singing, poetry and rapping, and it included a diverse amount of production. I didn't care if people didn't like it because, after all, I'd be dead anyway so criticism didn't matter.

The first song on the album was called "The Middle" and it was a spoken word song that explored the theory behind my life and posed the question: "Why does it have to end in the middle?"

The entire album would not be a "suicide album" until the last track on the last line, where I'd quit rapping in the middle of a song that sounds inspiring, and say, "Forget it, I'll just off myself right now," and then cut the song off with a record scratch. I posted the entire concept on my private Tumblr. This was a mistake.

It was November 18, 2015, that my parents found out about my plan. My father asked me if I was sad. I refused to answer the question.

"Son, we know about your plan. We know about this album and this plan you have to kill yourself and we are not letting it happen. We love you and have so much faith in you. We know life is tough but we just want to help," Dad said with a stern voice.

My father always meant well, and I loved him for it. In this instance, I took what he said as an attack rather than a father genuinely caring about his son. Stupid ol' narcissistic Lucas Sterling.

I agreed to delete everything I'd made for the album and gave up my phone for a couple nights as punishment. In this time of solitude, I realized that I did not want to die just yet. I realized I could just avoid being sad. This tactic of avoidance was a key point in my ultimate demise.

WHAT I DID TO MYSELF

On my birthday, Emma went out with me
and my family to a fancy restaurant. She got
me an oversized **pink** crewneck from Urban
Outfitters and a card with a nice note. I
turned 15 and we ate cake and I "celebrated"
another year on Earth.

After my birthday, I fell back into the
deep depression I was trapped in. That was
the last time for nearly 40 days that Emma
and I didn't argue. Sometimes, I still think
about how beautiful she looked and how
genuinely beautiful that night was. Then I
remember that my relationship with Emma
was toxic.

I was never really "afraid" to do anything;
in fact, I was known as fearless when it came
to expression. This changed when I met
Emma. I constantly ran from and avoided

things and stayed away from a lot of good people I loved because of Emma's undying jealousy and need for every piece of my attention every second that I was awake. My mind had been programmed to believe it saw Emma in everything; otherwise, I'd have made her angry by thinking about myself or something else too much.

I realized that my relationship with Emma was entirely too toxic on the 3rd of December when Emma wouldn't let me go out to dinner with Kyle for his birthday. It was a tradition we'd followed for as long as I'd known him. Every year we'd dress up like bums or little kids and go to an expensive restaurant and piss off all of the management with our appearance. I was going to dress the most "thug-like" and pay for everyone's meals this year.

"If you actually go, I don't even know why you're with me. You're supposed to drop everything for the people you love," Emma said with a slight bit of an attitude.

"And I love Kyle. He's basically been a brother to me for 10 years. No way I'll miss his birthday dinner, I never have," I spoke back, with a **smirk** because I thought I'd won.

"I'm leaving you if you don't reassess what you're doing tonight," Emma says sternly.

So that's how it was. I had to cancel my plans with my best friend to go to the mall with Emma that night, and burn a hole in my wallet that was intended for Kyle's dinner. I can't exactly complain about the last fact though. I bought her a **pink thong** that I really liked.

I was rich, white, and from the suburbs. Everything was cut out for me if I'd just conform to following it. I was always hesitant to buy things for myself with my own money, rather than for other people. Unless it were **cigarettes**. I'd quickly buy someone a pair of shoes or a phone case if they needed one, but I'd go on with a naked phone if *I* needed one. I definitely wasn't humble by a long shot, but I wasn't greedy with anyone but myself. That is the worst kind of greed.

Christmas 2015 was a fun time for Emma and I as individuals. The fighting had come to a halt, as I said it would around the holidays. My Aunt Caroline came into town and I was so happy I got to introduce her to Emma. Aunt Caroline thought Emma was cute but, with my best interest in mind, she told me to be careful.

"Just be safe. Girls like that will break your heart. You will understand one day," she said calmly.

I *chose* to act puzzled by this, though deep down I wanted to tell my aunt how sad I was. Aunt Caroline left and I wouldn't see her again until the summer, when we'd go to New York together.

Emma's birthday was a few days after Christmas, and I chose to go all out. For Christmas, I had gotten her a charm bracelet with a bunch of charms that represented the things we'd done together. I also got her parents a gift card to Dinner Royale. For Emma's birthday, I got her a meet-and-greet and VIP access to her favorite rapper, F-Hard, and a signed photo book from her favorite singer, The Weekdey. When Emma opened her presents, her response was … iffy. Surprisingly, she was mad at me because she thought I'd bought her these expensive things to "outdo" her presents.

"You know I don't have money like you do. Why do you always have to be so extravagant and one up me all the time?" Emma yelled at me in front of her whole family.

"Emma, you should be thanking Lucas. He just made two of your dreams come true," Pete, her father, said.

I knew I'd done nothing wrong, but again, I relied too much on what Emma thought. I immediately felt guilty for making Emma so angry. A wave of sadness and anger bounced over me. Emma was so rude and I was extremely tired of it. I got up and left. Pete came chasing after me, but I started sprinting. I was on the road, and before I knew it, I'd run three miles back to my house. Emma began calling me and screaming. Loudly.

"Why are you so fucking dramatic all the time?" she said.

Every time Emma yelled at me, I felt every scar on my body open back up and I felt salt rain from the sky. I was a cutting board, my feelings were a piece of meat, Emma was the butcher, and her words were a knife.

The route I took to fix this situation was unorthodox. It caught Emma by surprise. All I said on the phone was:

"I'm sorry. It won't happen again."

My new plan for combatting the enemy in this war was to succumb to all of her wishes. Typically, I'd never even associate with the enemy. But, with a love as toxic as ours, association with the enemy was ironically your own lifeline.

Emma and I were definitely thought of as a strong couple online, just like I was as an individual. But when people saw us offline, they realized we were a train wreck.

On New Year's Eve, Emma and I went to a kickback with her Somberton friends. We argued all evening because Emma didn't want me to do any drugs but she wanted me to give her permission to smoke. I had been doing drugs behind Emma's back for weeks leading up to this, so this was the first instance of me wanting to do drugs that she had seen. I decided I'd take a **Xanax** before meeting with Emma at her house. Stupid decision. I had started back on **Xanax** when winter break came around because I didn't want to remember the fighting I'd imagined would happen. Bad decision. I also started snorting **cocaine** to keep me focused on writing and working. Bad decision.

Emma was studying for the semester exam when I walked into her room. She immediately knew I was on something and she was not happy.

"I bought some weed for you," I said, pulling an eighth out of my back pocket.

"Really, Lucas?" Emma started. "Thank you for the weed, now leave. I don't want to see you like you are right now," she said after snatching it up.

"I can't help it. I think I'm addicted. I keep telling myself that this is my last one and then I do it again. I'm sorry," I said with genuine heartache.

I couldn't figure out why I'd been in such rough shape but it really scared me and everyone around me. I'd lost 17 pounds since I'd started doing drugs again. Emma didn't respond to this, so I tried to start a new conversation.

"What exam are you studying for?" I asked.

"Math. I told you this yesterday," Emma said. "Dammit, Lucas, you see what this shit does to you?" She started crying.

I immediately felt bad. I wanted to hold Emma but I felt that if I did, she'd say more terrible things. I didn't want to be addicted to drugs. I didn't want to hurt her anymore.

"Come here," I said softly. "I love you. I'm going to ease off the **xans and coke**. It isn't healthy. I'm sorry. You're still my girl, right?"

"**Xans *and* coke**? Lucas, you're going to end up killing yourself. Stop playing these games. Please. I can't watch this happen to you," Emma said.

Coke was easy to quit; it was not a drug that I enjoyed alone unless I was writing. I did not have the same luck in my prospect to lay off the **Xanax**. I just became more addicted to it the more I was withdrawn from it.

I started back at Drivestone on January 21st, 2016. I'd come into the second semester of freshman year taking two sophomore classes. My first day was horrendous. I didn't tell anyone, except Emma, that I'd be returning to Drivestone, because I wanted to surprise everyone. I didn't even tell my friends back at LAA that I was leaving. The situation was not handled very well, and I'd come to regret putting myself into it in the first place.

That first day people were all over me, shouting my name when they saw me and asking to take pictures. One girl even asked me if she could get my autograph. Drivestone had been paying attention to me after all. I had become an important boy.

I became *the* boy.

I BECAME THE BOY

I heard the name of Tim Tylers slide from Emma's mouth for the first time on January 22nd, 2016. I was not a fan from the beginning. It was a windy day, and Emma and I were walking from third block to our last classes of the day.

"Tim Tylers is counting down the days he has before he's 18 and unable to have sex with me," Emma randomly proclaimed with a **smirk** – *my* **smirk**

Emma loved the feeling she got when she made me feel like I was competing with someone. She always laughed at my jealousy.

"Why are you associating with him?" I automatically got defensive.

"He's my new friend. He's just a flirt; you don't need to worry about him," Emma said carelessly.

"You always choose the best friends," I said back with a hint of hurt.

Emma knew how to make things seem less important than they were and it was not fair. I had every right to be upset about Tim, but Emma acted as if I had no valid reasoning behind my feelings. I don't even believe you need reasoning for feeling. It's human nature.

I decided to do my homework on this Tim Tylers fellow and figure out his psyche. What I found was something I didn't expect to find.

Tim Tylers was committed to a second-rate college on a scholarship for football. Tim *also* was dating someone, a girl named Megan McDonald. I was sick. I had a vision that day in which I saw Tim destroy my relationship with Emma. I was panicking even though I thought I may have been overreacting.

I was not overreacting. Tim got Emma's Snapchat and began snapchatting her and they started a snapstreak. He apparently "laid off" of Emma, or at least that is what Emma claimed. I decided to try and drop everything that was I was stressing about. Emma promised nothing would happen. I had horses in my head.

Gallop, gallop, gallop, JUMP! Repeat.

I was slipping into insanity.

The F-Hard concert was six days after I transferred to Drivestone, and Emma talked about it every chance she got. I never was a bitter person but in this moment, I was. Why did Emma get to meet her hero but I had to wait god knows how long to meet mine? That is what I asked myself a billion times in the days leading up to the concert.

The concert came. Emma cried. I loved it, in the moment. We listened to music and we danced and we cried. We drove two hours to see him and I had never seen anyone as happy as Emma was when F went on stage. It was beautiful, I admit. I'd never felt so happy to see someone else happy. The concert was mediocre at best, once you think about it after. But, F's opener, R$VP, was really cool. I jumped a lot to his music.

I slept with my head on Emma's shoulder on the way back to our town that night. I was watching credits roll the whole time. This was going to be the last time I would see Emma appreciate me like this. I sensed it. I started writing down in my brain a plan for how I'd handle the situation when Emma left.

Emma sent naked pictures to Tim Tylers for the first time on Valentine's Day. I didn't find out for another month. She called Tim daddy and made plans to have sex with him. All I'd done that day was work to make her dinner, clean the house and decorate the dining room for her. We had sex that night, but we both felt the lust crawling on our skin. We knew this was poisonous but we didn't care anymore. I was utterly in love with Emma; I knew that. I wouldn't have left her had I known about the incident with Tim before I did, which we will get to, because I couldn't imagine being away from her.

Ironically, the strongest month of our relationship was the month of Valentine's Day. The reasoning for this was our mutual sex drives. Sex became a constant; we had it 56 times in the month of February alone. (She kept count of this with an app on her phone that tracks her ovulation cycles.)

This rapid sex fest stopped after a condom broke. I borrowed money from a friend and got Emma the Plan B pill and she was fine and never ended up pregnant, but it made the both of us more aware of how serious our relationship was. I had almost made a human being with Emma. That instance stayed stuck on my heart for months after.

I started gaining power and leveling up after releasing a writing called "To Anyone Who Cares," which talked about love, politics and how I was scared of the future. My hero, Tony Pillar, retweeted it. I later printed the copy of it out and thumbtacked it to my wall.

When Tony retweeted my writing, I knew I could write. I gained a thousand Twitter followers off of "To Anyone Who Cares." In my town, I blew up. I did what I'd dreamt of for months with one single writing. Secretly, Emma despised this. She wanted something to bring me back down to Earth. She thought my ego was flying too high. It was.

Emma got what she wanted early in March when I found out about her sending nude photos to Tim Tylers on Valentine's Day. My friend, Rayley Schmidt, told me. She was close with all of Tim's friends and she showed me the screenshots of Emma's nudes that Tim secretly kept and sent to all of his friends in a group chat. I cried for six hours and did not sleep. My original plan was to not even approach Emma about it, and just ignore it so I didn't lose her. Emma sensed something was wrong the minute she saw me at school the day after, and she picked my brain until I admitted what was going on.

"I just saw screenshots of Tim sending around naked pictures that he's received." I paused. "A lot of them were of you, and the timestamp said February 14th."

I began sobbing.

Without a word, Emma turned around and walked away.

I was ready to die right there, and had I had the opportunity, I would have. I threw my breakfast up in the bathroom, and cried my eyes out. Emma didn't speak to me until the end of the day, and she made every effort to avoid me.

"You're such a shitty boyfriend if you believe screenshots over me. Yeah, Tim and I flirt, and he touches me a lot, but I never sent him anything so stop being so fucking emotional." Emma snapped at me before leaving for her bus, "We are over. I swear to God, we are over."

I was dumped for the first real time in my life, right there. Of course, Emma and I had gotten into fights before and she'd "left," but something told me that this time, she wouldn't be back so soon.

CLOUT: THE BIGGEST MURDERER

A week later, I had a bad problem with thinking about death. Emma had sort of given me a chance to prove myself as trusting, though I knew I didn't have to. I had every reason to believe legitimate screenshots from a person who had never crossed me. Emma didn't think so.

Trance announced a rescheduled date for his tour for the end of March at a much larger venue than he'd been slated to perform at the first time. I knew his power was growing and it made me extremely happy because he deserved it over any other artist. I bought five tickets for all my "friends", and two meet and greets for Emma and I. I hoped this would show Emma that I didn't see us actually ending soon, not that I wanted to buy her back.

I began to believe that my relationship with Emma would end up in a book somewhere considering all the problems we faced. I started writing one, a collection of all of my poems and other writings that were all based off of my relationship with Emma. I didn't tell anyone about it until I got serious with it.

The yearly poetry competition held at my school came along and I decided I'd preview one of the better selections from my book there. It was titled "Floaties." It was a poem that compared my love for Emma to the effect of what floaties do for kids learning how to swim. I based it all off of a quote made by Tony Pillar: "The only way to learn to swim is without floaties."

I made it through rounds 1 and 2 of the competition easily. The final round came up, and it was in front of the *entire* school. I changed a few lines in the poem and decided I'd use it as a way to get Emma back, because everyone knew she was who the poem was about.

The competition came and I. Killed. It. The line that generated the standing ovation that I received was "The first time I kissed you, I saw the rest of my life flash before my eyes." While saying that line, I turned around to the opposite side of the room, where Emma was sitting, and started crying. That line triggered screams and tears and the biggest applause from my peers that I had seen in all of my life. I knew I was making waves. I saw it on the faces of everyone when I sat down and people were still standing for me, screaming, "Encore! Encore! Encore!"

Unfortunately, I did not win the competition because a group of seniors who'd done the competition and lost every year since they came into high school were rewarded for their efforts throughout every semester. The judges, all of them teachers at my school, had to give the award to that group and I was okay with it. I knew I had the best poem though. And so did the rest of my school. "Floaties" is what made me realize I really was leveling up. I'd never seen anyone openly cry because of my words before, but I loved it. Evoking emotion was my best skill and I was ready to use it.

I tweeted a video of "Floaties" and it blew up. I received thousands more followers off of it. I was the talk of everyone around me. I couldn't go out to dinner with my family without someone asking if I was Lucas

Sterling, "the deep guy from Twitter." I had always been popular in school due to my wittiness, but I'd never imagined I'd be approached over 20 times a day for a week straight with compliments and stories of how "Floaties" affected people.

Emma was still bitter at the fact that I had been gaining more and more attention. What was funny about the situation was, no matter how badly Emma acted like she didn't want me, she took me back with open arms. After "Floaties," I was *the* Lucas Sterling and she had no choice but to take me back. I had written a love ballad about her and people from all over the world had watched it.

The day of the Trance concert, Emma let me smoke weed on the condition that I buy the weed and she got to smoke with me. I was fine with that as long as she didn't screw me over at the last minute. We linked up at our friends house with the three others whose tickets I bought, Ian Thomas, Kelly Trace (Kell), and Kimberly Rodgers. They were three of my closest friends since 8th grade and it was because of me that they even knew Trance's name. Kell's mom dropped us off at the concert, and Emma and I had to leave the group to go to our meet and greet. I was really nervous and I chain smoked an entire pack of

Newports while waiting to meet Trance. I wore all black, and my shirt had the emblem of Trance's latest album, *ShroomSongs,* on it. It was colorful and I knew Trance would like that. Kell, Kimberly, and Ian got fastpass tickets and they held our drugs for us while we went into the venue. In return, we told them we'd save them a spot since we'd be the first to be in the venue after the meet and greet ended.

I met my hero at the end of March, 2016. I told him that he saved my life and he responded humbly, telling me that I had no idea but I'd saved his also. Trance was and will always be the most important human being to ever enter my life and stay. The concert changed my life. I watched him laugh and smile and do a remix to his favorite children's song. I cried a lot, I danced a lot, and I kissed Emma a lot. It was magical and colorful. I received a signed poster, I was front row the entire time, and I could not stop screaming. I barely smoked any weed because I wanted this moment to be the real Lucas Sterling, not a drug infested Lucas Sterling. I crowd surfed and nearly got kicked out of the venue for it, but Trance shouted me out on stage when he saw me. Life was a coloring book at the start of that day, and I filled it all up by the end of the night. I don't even know why I'm writing about this, considering it was the one moment that I know for sure I will *never* be able to fully explain in words.

My parents and I began drifting apart as I became closer to Emma's parents. Pete knew of my depression through Emma and we began talking regularly. I didn't tell him the extent of my problems, because he would have pushed for me to be admitted to a facility, but I opened up to him a lot. Emma and I began talking to her mother, Annie, and we'd all cook dinner together and I'd tell them how I felt more at home around them than anyone else.

It was mid April when I became dangerously addicted to popping any kind of **pill** I could get my hands on. I preferred **Xanax and Valium** but I'd take at least five **Benadryl** a day to help me feel out of touch with reality. I was tired of walking without a purpose, so I wanted to breathe without one. I had felt like a failure because I couldn't just create something without hating it five seconds later. It was a low in my life that I'd never thought I would experience. A lot of my peers got onto the **Xanax** wave that spring, but none abused it as terribly as I did.

The problem with **Xanax** was memory loss. It helped me with writing because it pushed me to describe everything I saw while barred out (meaning high on **Xanax**) in deep detail, so that I'd know exactly what happened the next day. Emma had no knowledge of my drug usage, and was oblivious to the fact that I would sometimes be completely barred out at school without her even knowing.

I hated myself. I knew this to be true because, secretly, every time I took a pill, I had a sliver of hope that it would kill me. My hope was almost granted on May 3rd. I took **15 Benadryl, 2 bars of Xanax and a few Ibuprofen** on a Tuesday morning before school. I knew I was going to die that day. I got on the bus and went about my daily routine. When I saw Kyle before the first class in the morning, I hugged him and told him I loved him. I kissed Emma six times on our way to biology that morning, and Emma knew right away that something was wrong. She just didn't know how serious it was. She thought I was going through another one of my depressed phases, not that I was trying to kill myself.

Emma went to the bathroom that morning to touch up her makeup, and when she came back, she discovered that I had fallen asleep on my desk. I have no recollection of anything past me walking into the room, so this is all based on what I was told. Emma tried to wake me, but was unsuccessful. After reporting this to the teacher, Emma and my peers had come to the conclusion that I had had a seizure. After confirming with my mom that I did not have epilepsy, Emma put two and two together and realized I had been acting off that morning because I'd taken drugs.

I, Lucas Sterling, woke up in an ambulance with no recollection of anything that had happened that morning. I had no idea what *was* happening or what *had* happened. I remember seeing the tears in my mom's eyes as the EMTs rushed me to the emergency room. I remember asking what happened and having to be told four times before I understood the fact that I had tried to kill myself. I remember wondering if Emma was okay. I just didn't remember anything that happened after I'd stepped onto the bus that morning. This troubled me very much. I knew that whatever happened must have happened in first block, because the clock in the ambulance said it was only 8:47 a.m.

Six thousand milliliters of water later, I was alive and well. Then, after the most traumatic experience of my life, I was told that my suicidal ideations and drug abuse were cause for me to go to a mental health institution and let them keep me for a week to "evaluate" me. I was already taking 10mg of **Prozac** a day and I felt that to be more than enough for me. Regardless, I was put into handcuffs and taken away from my family on May 5th, and shipped 3 hours away to a facility.

Henry Hillow Children's Behavioral and Mental Health Facility, Henry Hillow for short, was the closest I have ever been to believing in a Heaven and Hell. You can probably guess which destination I felt I was at for a week. I was able to get Emma put on the call list by pretending she was my sister. I was allowed two phone calls a day, and I'd call Emma once a day to figure out how things were going. Everyone knew what I had done and they all had their own opinions on why I did it. That made me scared for school. I decided I'd get serious with the poetry book while in the hospital so that when I was released, I could publish it and clear the air. I wrote six things in the first day. I cried a lot while I was hospitalized. I thought I'd discovered God in the first couple of days, until I realized on day 3 that I still had four days left in Hell.

"God shouldn't ground you," I ranted to one of the behavioral health technicians on my fifth day there.

"I know, but it's life. You gotta roll with it or you'll get run over," the man spoke back.

His nametag said "Bryan" but I wanted to believe it really said "Steve" because he reminded me of the guy from Blue's Clues. Anyway, I took a liking to Bryan because I related to him. He knew I was sad and knew that at the end of the day, nothing can cure sadness, only prolong it. Henry Hillow believed too much in coping skills being a savior to mankind, rather than believing in combatting things. They didn't teach you how to get rid of your sadness, just how to let it stack up. Plus, no kid could get terrible news one day and then say, "Oh, well, I suppose I should do my breathing exercises." I wasn't a fan of this hospital because of these opinions.

The psychiatrist at the hospital, Dr. Leaders, was only in his medical practice to make money. He did not care about kids. He spoke to each kid individually for about five minutes at most. He smelled like Axe cologne and his hair was always gelled up and curled at the ends. I did not like him but I played along with everything he said for the limited time I had with him each day.

As promised, I was released a week after I was admitted, on a Wednesday. The four-hour car ride home was very fun for me. Being locked inside for a week really killed me, so I rode most of the way home with my window cracked. I'd never been more grateful to smell the factory smoke smell of my hometown.

As soon as I was out, I texted Emma: "I'm out :)"

She immediately responded with six messages explaining how happy she was and how much she loved and missed me.

I tweeted: "Hello. I missed you. I'm sorry," and received several retweets in seconds. Everyone had missed me, too, and they'd turned my tweet notifications on so that as soon as I was free, they would see my tweet. They missed my problematic opinionated view of everything and my stray writings and sweet pictures and tweets about Emma.

I went to school the next day and was greeted with a bombardment of questions and hugs from people. Everyone was asking if I was okay and if I needed anything and saying they were happy I was well. I began crying when I saw the amount of love that I'd been shown by my peers. I saw Emma for the first time since I'd gotten home due to my parents forcing me to go to my church youth group. I was so ecstatic to see Emma at school and we were set to hang out after at her house.

When Emma walked into the student center at Drivestone that morning, it felt like the entire world stopped to watch how things would develop. I dropped my chocolate muffin on the floor and began running toward Emma, and she was wrapped up in my arms in seconds. When we kissed, everyone in the room turned and smiled. More magical moments were happening to me in a matter of weeks than had happened to me in the first 14 and a half years of my life.

After school, at Emma's house, I was greeted with three warm hugs from Annie, Pete and Emma's grandmother, who was in town visiting from New Jersey. I felt like, for once, I was where I belonged.

My pill popping and drug habits burnt out. I was tired of relying on everything else to give me satisfaction. I still used **cigarettes** as my anxiety medication because nobody at the hospital would prescribe me anything. I knew that satisfaction was only genuine if I sought it in the right way. I was tired of setting limits for my real passion so I stopped underestimating myself and grew wings. I wanted to go to the end of the world and meet the devil and write a book about it. Little did I know, my entire relationship with Emma was actually stitched into that plot idea from the beginning.

I reached out to Michelle Minson, the girl who was with Emma the night of the accident, toward the end of May. She was close friends with Rayley Schmidt (the girl who had told me about the Tim Tylers incident), so we got along well. Spontaneous friendships were all a part of the syllabus I set up for my new life. I developed a new feeling of trust and belief in people who did not deserve it. Michelle ended up trying to get me to sleep with her, which I gladly would have, but it would have made me a hypocrite. Ray and I remained close after that, but Michelle had no interest in me if I wasn't going to have sex with her. She had never been turned down before.

Rayley did not like Emma. She was a good friend and knew how terribly Emma treated me and knew that it wasn't fair. She begged me to leave Emma and go out and be happy. Months later, Rayley ended up confessing that she had secret feelings for me and was jealous of Emma for getting me.

Emma was not a fan of Rayley either. I found this out one day after Rayley tweeted that I was a good person and people need to treat me how I deserved.

"You're becoming friends with her? You're such a joke lol," Emma texted me.

"We were just having a conversation earlier when she needed someone. Why is that so bad?" I shot back.

"You obviously can't tell that she has major feelings for you. She never leaves you alone and she wants everyone to believe that *I'm* the bad one in this relationship," Emma said.

"Are you saying I am the bad one?" I asked.

"I may be alluding to what the world thinks. You aren't a good person, babe," Emma said.

This argument with Emma upset me. A lot. I wanted to do drugs and get back at her. I ended up meeting up with Rayley and her friend, Madeline, and we all smoked weed in Madeline's car after going to a sketchy kickback. I did not tell Emma afterward because I knew she'd leave and I realized it was a mistake. I just wanted to live my life for once without having to worry about what Emma thought. I had a good time. I didn't have sex or kiss or even flirt with Madeline or Rayley, and I know this to be true because I remember every vivid detail of that night. We all just had a good time and talked about music and our lives.

Madeline could not drive me home that night because she was too high so I had to get a ride from my new friend, Megan McDonald. That's right; the Megan that dated Tim Tylers. She had recently reached out to me because she knew about the Tim incident and wanted to tell me that she was sorry that he was the way he was. Megan was popular and cool so I figured it was good for high school politics to have her on my side.

I went to a party the next night. Emma still didn't know that I'd gone out the night before, and I was trying to keep it that way. This was my first "real" high school party with alcohol and drugs all around me. A lot of people showed up. Emma didn't go because she was hanging out with a friend who had moved away but was back into town for a week. Tim was at the party. I didn't know it, but Tim was telling Emma everything that had happened with me the night before. I had been thrown under the bus that I should have never boarded.

A VERY WARM SUMMER

Emma broke up with me within minutes of hearing about my night with Rayley and Madeline. She then sent very erotic pictures and messages to Tim Tylers because she wanted a way to get back at me. Tim was now 18 and he made plans to have sex with Emma and sent her nude photos in return. Tim Tylers had the intent to commit statutory rape and he sent inappropriate pictures of himself to a 15-year-old girl.

The next day, Emma decided to get back together with me when she received proof that I had not had sex or done anything disloyal with the girls. She came over, looked me in my eyes and told me she loved me and cared about me more than anything. Emma did not tell me she was planning to have sex with Tim at this time. I would not find that out for two months.

After this incident, I told Emma that she could not continue to leave my life and then come back to me when it was convenient for her. I told her that I would not take her back next time. This only made her angrier.

"You were out there doing God knows what with Rachel and Madeline, but you're mad at me?" Emma asked.

The irony. I still laugh at the fact that she was concerned about Rayley for months, and made me cut her off although I never even did *anything* with her. But if I asked her to cut Tim off, I'd get screamed at.

"I'm not mad, I just find it funny how you can leave me when you're mad and then get back together with me when you're happy," I stated calmly.

"Okay, Lucas, the next time you pull some shit like this, it's over. End of story," Emma said.

"Ok, Emma." I responded with a **smirk**.

June came around and Emma and I started doing well again. I had to stop talking to Rayley after the incident, a rule that Emma would not budge on whatsoever. I didn't think a relationship should have rules as much as expectations, but Emma constantly called everything a rule. I was not allowed to have Snapchat streaks with other girls, so I had to Snapchat certain people every other day. I was not allowed to go out to a party or go anywhere with friends unless Emma was there. This was due to my "drug problem" that was still destroying me, Emma claimed. I hate being told that I have a drug problem just because I tried to kill myself. Like, yeah, the situation I put myself into wasn't right, but I didn't need to go to rehab for it. I was a 15-year-old boy living his life and experiencing high school like any other 15-year-old.

Regardless of anything I said, Emma was always right in her own eyes and nothing could change that. I was not allowed to disagree with her in a conversation, no matter how wrong she was. Nothing, not logic nor reason, could bring Emma to admit her wrongs. I would bring Emma **flowers** and milkshakes and she'd complain that I did not get her the right color of **rose** or her favorite milkshake flavor (which I swear to God changed every other week).

June was not a bad month though, in the grand scheme of things. I started working on my EP, a sort of "half-album" I planned to release on my birthday. The friend from out of town that Emma had been with a month before, Caitlin, was back in town from Mississippi. I came over to Emma's house, where Caitlin was staying for a few nights while she was in town, to hang out. I brought my camera so I could take pictures of them, and they both asked me to direct them in modeling. I had recently gotten serious about photography so this was the perfect time to use my camera for this situation.

The girls were naturals, and they ended up posting one of the pictures I took of them together. Emma and I also took some pictures together, after I trained Caitlin for 30 minutes on how to use the camera and correct brightness and all other aspects before trusting her to take pictures of us. They turned out well. My favorite was one of me holding Emma close to my face and I edited that in black and white and posted it on Instagram along with the first picture we'd ever taken together, back at the football game in September. I captioned the throwback picture "I like to look back at this moment," and the current picture "I like to live in this one." It was definitely the cutest thing I'd ever done.

I went to the beach alone the next week. I suppose I wasn't alone, because I had family there with me. But I felt pretty lonely. The beach is where I finished writing my collection of poetry. I released it on the day that I came back from the beach. It was free online but a lot of people bought hard copies, 107 people to be specific. I made over $500 in a week off of that book, titled "I've Become Counterproductive." It was a hit, though I quickly became less of a fan of it than most people were. I constantly analyzed that book after its release and decided that I should have made the theme a little stronger. A lot of the writings were about having your heart broken, and Emma didn't take that very kindly. I wrote IBC from the perspective of my friends and other people I know.

"This is terrible, Lucas. I can't believe you'd put our relationship out there like that. If you keep making yourself look like a joke, I will make sure to ruin you," Emma said to me sternly after reading the poem in which I compared past stories of a relationship to objects for sale at a garage sale.

"It was just some art I felt like kids needed to hear," I said back, trying to remain calm while knowing my rationality only went so far when someone degraded something I was proud of. The book wasn't perfect, but it was well written and deserved some type of respect.

"Whatever, I just can't wait for someone to call you out for your irresponsibility. You're a terrible boyfriend and again, you are *not* a good person, so stop pretending. Nobody cares about your little book," Emma snapped.

"Maybe if you weren't such a rude person all my writings about you would be like *Floaties*!" I snapped back. I was done with this. Nobody was going to take my sanity away.

Emma walked away. She then told me to go. I wouldn't do it though, because I knew I messed up by yelling. I immediately began apologizing. We lay in bed together without saying a word for hours. Finally, I spoke.

"Look, I didn't mean to ..." I started but was interrupted by Emma's lips shuttling from my lips to my neck to little nibbles on my ear. I kissed back and once again, our utopian relationship was governed and constituted by sex.

Sex pushed Emma and me to a state we'd never felt before. The way our bodies intertwined so beautifully was intensely euphoric. Our favorite songs came out in the form of moans and intense gasps for air. The only time Emma let herself be vulnerable was when her clothes were off; she was unpredictable at that point. Emma Illiano and I, Lucas Sterling, were only in love in bed. In the real world, we were enemies.

I went to New York early in July to see the Broadway show that helped inspire my need for writing. It was a musical about the life of a political figure in America and how he became such an important part of American history. This man wrote non-stop, much like I did, and he also spoke too much and it got him in trouble a lot, much like me. I identified with this man. Seeing the musical live was a dream come true for me. It was dreamy and amazing and definitely the greatest show to take the Broadway stage in years.

The show was a dream come true, but what happened afterward was what really changed my life. I gave a copy of my poetry book to the star and writer of the musical, and I hugged him. I couldn't even say anything because I was so shocked to have the opportunity to speak to the man. My aunt had lined up this short meet and greet because she was and forever will be the biggest legend in my family when it came to making someone's dream come true. If I could be half of the person that she is, and care as much about generosity as she does, I'd make it by.

I texted Emma immediately and she pretended to be happy for me: "That's really cool, babe. I hope he likes it!" she said back to my all caps, multiple misspelling-filled text.

The hotel I stayed at with my aunt was beautiful. It reminded me of the apartment building I'd want to live in one day. A beautiful shower with an urban stained window next to it, and an exposed brick wall behind the vanity in the bathroom. It was nothing less than amazing. I was happy for once in the city, but I was also ready to leave before I got too attached.

After New York, I realized I hadn't really been doing much besides sitting around the house. I was lazy and undedicated to my body. I decided I'd reach out to a senior named James Joshua, who was 18, to help me out in the gym. I wanted to get my body in shape so I'd feel less disgusting. I wasn't fat by any means. I was practically anorexic, and that was a problem. I had been eating two meals a day for a week straight, and it was very unhealthy. I watched my bones slowly begin to have more character than ever on my nude body.

I chose James because he was a fan of my work and I knew I'd be able to finesse free training sessions out of him. He consistently asked me for playlists and scrapped writings because he was heavily inspired by my work. He was almost obsessed, to be honest, and I'll admit that I didn't like it. It's weird to be treated as if you are almost superhuman, especially by kids who are older than you. A part of me reached out to James because I wanted him to realize that I was not really that different than him, because he was looking at me too much from a fanboy perspective.

James agreed to train me on one condition, which was that I make us a gym playlist. James was in a clique at the local gym called, "LC CREATED," short for "Lifestyle Connection Created," named after the gym, "Lifestyle Connection Fitness Center." Apparently, James had been going to that gym for a while, so he and his friends decided to make a collective of gym sharks who hashtagged their Instagram and Twitter photos "#LCCREATED" and sometimes went out to dinner together. I didn't understand, and I found it pretty corny, but I needed James to help me out, so I didn't say anything about it.

James was out of town for the next two weeks visiting his sick uncle in Pennsylvania, so he said we'd work when he was back. That didn't end up working for me because I was to be in Chicago the week that James was coming back. I decided I'd just catch James whenever he was available, and in the meantime go to the gym by myself and start my own diet plan. James didn't cross my mind for weeks.

Chicago. My favorite place to be on the entire Earth. I was at my best when I was away from the Drivestone environment, but even better when I was in my dreams. Chicago was the dream I lived in for months and months until the week I was scheduled to go every summer. I was to be attending my first music festival while there, Latona Fest. Trance wasn't performing there, but it was in Trance's hometown so I had a sliver of hope that I'd see him.

I got in contact with a few of my friends from Chicago who I knew would be at the fest, and decided I'd hang out with them. It was possibly the coolest and worst decision that I've ever made in my life. I rolled hard on **Molly** for the first time in my life while I danced like I was going to die that night at the

EDM stage. I felt so alive and so happy. My friends, Gretch, short for Gretchen, and Louis (pronounced loo-ee), were the coolest kids I'd ever met. They were a couple that had been together for nine months and all they cared about was living like they'd die the next day. They didn't seem to ever really have problems with each other, and that made me so jealous. I wished I'd had that. Their relationship reminded me of the song "Belong" by Ernest Soft and The Repellent Ones.

Emma worried sick every day that I was doing drugs at Latona and she told me she'd leave me if she found out I was on any. With this in the back of my head, I chose not to tell Emma about my trial run with **Molly** on day 1 of the four-day dream I was living. Bad decision, yes. But the less Emma knew, the better off she was.

I spent most of day 2 doing shrooms, something I discovered that day, and rolling off **molly** while tripping crazily at the EDM stage again. I was drawn to dancing that weekend and it really stayed with me afterwards. I went to one of the biggest artists at the festival's set around 7:30 p.m. to catch the last 15 minutes. The artist's name was Past and he was one of the most energetic musicians I had ever seen. I arrived and listened to Past play one of his bangers, "April Fools," and then to my surprise, Trance came out on stage.

"TRANCE!!!! I LOVE YOU, YOU SAVED MY LIFE. THANK YOU. I LOVE YOU SO MUCH!!!" I screamed while Trance performed one of his most well known songs, "You Don't Want These Problems." It was a dream come true for me. I was tripping off two drugs, listening to my favorite artist live, away from Drivestone, and with good people.

I was not satisfied with just hearing one song from Trance. I finessed my way backstage by spending all of my money in return for an artist pass, and waited at the gate for Trance to come out. I waited for three hours to no avail. I was discouraged. Suddenly, Josh Perc, a member of Trance's collective, came out of the artist tent.

"YO! Josh Perc! Come here!!" I yelled.

"What's up, my mans?" Josh asked.

"Listen, I am a huge fan of you, your entire collective in fact. Is Trance in that tent?" I asked.

"Yes sir, and I'm guessing you want to meet him." Josh smiled at me. He'd obviously been through this before.

"Please. Thirty seconds. You can take my phone and this will never be documented so you don't get in trouble." I begged.

I knew I looked like a joke, but I did not care. The high was speaking for me. I'd spent my entire allowance that I'd saved for weeks on this moment. I would not throw away my shot.

"Deal. Give your phone and bag to security," Josh said. "He's with me. Thirty seconds. Turn around." Josh slipped a $20 bill to the security guard.

"Whoa, whoa. You don't have to do that!" I exclaimed.

I was taken aback. Josh Perc, one of my favorite artists from Chicago, just bribed a security guard for the chance for a 15-year-old kid to meet his hero. I had to have been tripping super hard, or fate was not as bad as I had always thought it was at getting things right.

I thanked Josh six times on the way to the tent where the artists were.

"Listen, there's a lot of big names in here. The Weekdey, Past, and Big Layne are all here. You can't talk to them because you only have about a minute with Trance before a chick will pull him away. He is popping right now," Josh said very fast.

He talked to me in a tone that made me feel like we were friends. It was cool.

"Yes sir," I said with a salute.

Josh opened the flap of the tent, and I immediately started scanning my surroundings. I saw rapper and mogul Big C eating a corn dog and talking to the band Stereolegs. It was super insane and intense. I followed Josh to the back of the tent, where we sat on a plush couch and waited.

"He's probably talking to someone right now. Hov apparently stopped by so Trano probably went to go see if Auntie Bey was with him. My mind exploded. Auntie Bey and Hov just stopped by, and Trance was talking to them? This drove me nuts. Suddenly, someone tapped Josh on the shoulder and then sat down. I knew it was Trance as soon as I saw the hat branding his band, The Kid's Lab. The tears immediately rushed to my face and I choked up.

"Who's the kid?" Trance asked, smiling.

"Oh yeah, what's your name, dude?" Josh asks. "You never told me."

"Lucas. Lucas Sterling. Lucas Blaise Sterling," I respond. I had gotten to the smiling uncontrollably stage now.

"Lucas here is definitely your biggest fan. Dude literally stood back there for three hours just for the chance to meet you, haha. If it wasn't for me walking out to go to the stage, he would've probably sat out there for the rest of the night," Josh said.

"Wow, that's crazy, man. Hi, I'm Trance. It's really cool to meet you." Trance said and then dapped me up like a friend.

I hugged Trance. I did not and still do not care if this was too much, I had to do it.

"I spent all of the money in my wallet to buy some guy's artist pass just to get to the gate. I was determined to meet you. You saved my life. I told you that at the meet and greet you had in NC in March," I said with slurred words.

"Wow, dude. That's insane. Nobody has ever done that before, I don't think. Do you want to chill back here with us for the rest of the time? I'll introduce you to some people," Trance asked politely.

"Holy shit," was all I could say. The tears started welling up.

"His bag is with security. Can you send Paul to go get him cleared?" Josh asked. Paul was Trance's manager. I knew this because I knew everything about Trance.

"You guys are the greatest people I've ever met. Thank you so much. Wow," I said. I could not believe that this was happening.

I tried acid for the first time that night. Acid had been the motif for Trance's early career so it was easy for him to get. Trance did not do acid or any drugs anymore, though, because he had recently become a father, but he did still smoke **cigarettes** like a lot of other Chicago natives. **Cigarettes** and more **cigarettes**.

"I wanna be a good influence, not just for my kids, but for your kids. I had my fun in my youth, but I am 23 and have a daughter now. This shit is more serious than it was three years ago," Trance said to me.

"Man, I can't even express to you how I feel about your music. You have been the troublemaker, the kid who did the acid, and now you're the man with the baby and the key to the city of Chicago at 23. Why don't you seriously run for mayor?" I asked.

"I will eventually," Trance said. "I want to keep making music until I'm not able to inspire kids anymore, and then I'll run for mayor. I'm hoping to have saved the city before then though."

"Wow, man. Thank you so much for this night. I can't even begin to explain the number of times you've saved my life. When I'm sad, it's your shit I listen to. You've saved me from suicide multiple times."

"Wow, dude. You have no idea how much you and your devotion to my music means. That is crazy. Don't ever downplay yourself. You're a smart kid. You remind me a lot of myself," Trance said.

"I wrote a book this summer and I wanted to give you a copy," I said. I pulled the copy out of my bag and handed it to him.

"Will you sign it for me?" Trance asked politely. This was a God dream that I was living in at this point. There was no way that Trance the Trapper was asking for my autograph. I quickly opened the page and slowly scribbled my signature down along with a print of my Twitter username, with a little message saying, "I hope this is a blessing."

"You're going to die a legend, Lucas Sterling. I can't wait until you're back here with us one day for the entire show. Thanks for the vibes, big fella."

We took a picture together and that was what I was left with. Trance said his goodbyes and we walked our separate ways for what I hoped would not be long.

Trance followed me on Twitter that night.

"DRUG PROBLEM"

I woke up the next day and realized I was only halfway through the festival and all of my dreams had come true. I'd only gotten a couple of hours of sleep that night due to all the drugs in my system, so I didn't feel very ready for the day ahead of me. I decided against going to the festival on Saturday due to my exhaustion from the night before.

I slept all day. There were no artists I'd wanted to see on the Saturday lineup, so I wasn't missing anything. I ended up fighting with Emma because she thought I wasn't texting her enough.

"I literally was with my hero last night. Did you want me to text you every minute and be rude?" I asked. I had no more time for the stupidity of my relationship.

"I sent nudes to Tim after you went out with Rayley. He was the one who told me about it and I chose to send him nudes and videos to get back at you for that," Emma said out of nowhere, on the phone that night.

I had not expected this. I didn't know how to react. I was angrier at the fact that Emma told me this only because she wanted to bring me down, rather than because she was sorry.

"And you can't be mad at me because it was your fault. Had you not gone out, you wouldn't have had to deal with this. I hope you think next time. I called him daddy and made plans to do stuff with him. He was going to pick me up and take me back to his house the day that you and I got back together, but I turned him down once I realized I wanted to give you a chance," Emma said all at once.

"Okay," I say.

I did Adderall, Molly and smoked weed that night. I was completely off my ass. I'd linked up with all the new friends I'd met and we threw a penthouse party in The Rake Hotel. It was crazy. I did not care anymore. I had started a novel while on the plane ride to Chicago, and I knew I wouldn't finish it once I got home. I decided to write the ending down so that I'd be able to pass it on to the world. The book would end with the main character killing himself as a form of revenge on the girl that he loved for her not treating him right. I wrote down the rough draft and then passed out on Louis' couch.

I went to the last day of the fest the next day. I hadn't texted Emma in 12 hours, though I knew what she was doing. I partied hard all day. I met more new people, including girls, though I did not do anything with them because technically I was still dating Emma. One of my fans DM'd me on Twitter and asked to meet up and take a picture with me. Her name was Tina. She was short and wore a crop top, and was very drunk when we met up, like everyone else I was around.

Tina and I dropped acid at the stage where one of my favorite rappers, Vinnie Paper, was performing. I told her about Emma and that I was definitely going to break up with her the next day when I was sober. Tina and I didn't have any real connection past drugs and wanting to have a good time, except that Tina told me she'd do stuff with me if I ended up breaking up with Emma. She was very attractive and I told her I'd be fine with that, as long as I was single. Low of me, I know, but also payback in my eyes.

I met another girl at the last set of the day for the EDM Stage. Her name was Ann Marie. She was very nice and she knew me from Twitter also, and that's why she approached me. With all the people recognizing me, I knew I was leveling up. I was very happy. I split away from Gretchen and Louis to hang out with Ann Marie and her friend Kim. They were both Chicago natives and they lived just two blocks away from where I was staying. Ann Marie and Kim did Xans that night but I said no when they asked me if I wanted anything. I felt responsible and I knew my mom would be proud of me. I told them the entire plot for my novel. They were in love. Ann Marie's uncle was a publisher and she wanted to put in a good word for me. She texted me his number. Ann Marie was very curvy and beautiful and this made me want to see her more.

Gretchen and Louis came to snatch me up at the end of the show, so I asked Ann Marie and Kim if they'd meet up with us later that night at a party or something. They accepted my offer and Ann Marie gave me a hug and kiss on my cheek before getting in the Uber I'd called for them.

I realized I really was making waves. Ann Marie marked the sixth person to recognize me at the fest. Two of those six seemed to be down with having sex with me. I knew I was never going to fail. I called Emma and ended things with her. I was very high, but I knew if I didn't let the drugs talk for me I'd probably never actually do what I needed to do. I pretended I was sober. Emma believed me.

"We are over. I am tired. You do not love me; you love the idea of being in control. I gave you the chance to meet your idols and you took advantage of my niceness. Go be with Tim. I'll be happy for you," I said as emotionless as possible.

"I should have let you die in May on that desk. I should have told the teacher you were just sleeping. You don't deserve to be alive," Emma said back. She was obviously drunk.

I cried. I knew this time it was really it. I would not go back. I would do anything to move on from Emma. I blocked her number after she went on a rant about how I don't deserve to be alive.

After I became a single man, Gretch, Louis, and I went to another penthouse party. This hotel was luxurious. Gretch said she'd never been inside but that I needed to dress nice. We decided to sell all our drugs to a couple friends of Louis and get nice outfits. There'd be drugs at the party anyways.

I bought a green bomber jacket, with a long black cardigan underneath, and a ripped shirt along with skinny jeans. They let us in and we took the elevator to the top floor, number 57. My name wasn't on the list but Gretch and Louis' were. They just said I was famous and the bouncer believed us because I was dressed like a corny famous model. Gretch bought a hotel room for us on the 16th floor. It was two bedroom and bathroom; it felt like a cozy apartment. This is when I figured out Gretch was rich.

The person hosting the party was friends with Josh Perc, and Josh came through. He introduced me to the host, a rapper named Lokio, and we kicked it and smoked for a bit. Lokio asked me to DJ after Josh told him that I had a crazy taste. I was never but accepted. I threw on a few songs by The Kooks and Jeff Rosenstock and even a Green Day song to troll all the kids there, then I dropped the beat to "April Fools" by Past and transitioned it into "Father Stretch My Hands Pt. 1." It was crazy. I was running on cocaine and molly for the rest of the night. Ann Marie showed up around 2 a.m. after I'd texted her and told her she had to come.

I wrapped my set around 3:30 after Ann Marie had been dancing like crazy but told me she was getting tired. I ended with a little transition from "No Flockin" by Kodak Black into "X" by 21 Savage into the "Lil Uzi Vert" intro to Young Thug's album, which then spun into the song "CD" by Trance The Trapper. It was bonkers and the kids there loved it.

Lokio paid me $1,500 and gave me a quarter ounce of cocaine and some molly. I bid him farewell and Ann Marie and I went back to my room around 4. We immediately shared an eight ball of coke. We took some of her Adderall to even the high out and avoid the depressant part. It worked.

I had Ann Marie in bed in 30 minutes with her clothes off. We did not hook up. We did other things, but I told her that I was not going to have sex with her and she understood. After we'd finished making out, we laid in bed naked. She told me she was in love with me but I knew it was just the drugs talking. That's all it ever was.

I hung out with Ann Marie, Gretch and Louis, and a couple other people for the few days after Latona ended. I left on Wednesday and they were all crying. They told me I was the coolest 15-year-old they'd met, and that I needed to come up again soon. I told them I would be honored to see them soon. They all wished me well with my novel, and told me they wanted signed copies when it released. I gave Ann Marie a kiss on her forehead and told her I'd see her soon.

On the plane ride home, I wrote about my entire experience in the notes on my iCloud library. I wrote about every day in deep detail. I wanted to make a short story out of it all one day.

The day I got home, I realized how much my life sucked at home. I'd just experienced the best week ever, and now I had to detox. I was having withdrawals from the molly and the coke, and that was driving me crazy. I asked my friends for some but they wouldn't sell to me. I was confused as to why.

I began getting very serious about my novel. I locked myself in my room one day and wrote the entire storyboard on my chalkboard wall. I felt like a genius. I knew it would help kids and also help me. I decided I would not kill myself until after it was released.

One afternoon, my mother walked into my room while I was writing, and accused me of a lot of things.

"I just got off the phone with Emma. Why didn't you tell us you broke up with her?" my mom asked.

"It wasn't important," I responded.

"I'm going to need you to pee in a cup."

"What?" I shot back. How could she know?

"Pee in a cup and open the notes on your phone right now," my mother said. "I'm not playing around, Lucas."

It all clicked. I had given Emma my iCloud password a few weeks back so that all of my information backed up to her computer. She must have seen the notes on my phone about my time in Chicago and told my mom. I was beyond livid. This also explained why nobody would sell me drugs; she was telling everyone I had a "drug problem."

"I hope you know that bitch didn't tell you any of that because she cared. She said it because she wants to spite me," Lucas says.

"She also read to me some other notes. It sounds like you're back at square one. You're talking about suicide a lot. You need help, Lucas," my mother said.

"Wait, wait. No. I admit, I did a lot of drugs in Chicago but I don't have a 'problem' and I don't write about suicide. She's lying. I swear," I said.

That did not stop my mom from talking to my therapist.

I was admitted to a hospital 45 minutes away from my house that Friday, August 14th. Emma Illiano had succeeded in ruining my life. Nobody believed my side of the story. Everyone thought I'd just deleted all my notes so I wouldn't have to serve in-patient time. I was in the hospital for five days.

I was admitted into a unit with five girls and one boy. I woke up on day 1 to a nice man named Marcus calling my name for breakfast. Mr. Marcus was the man who reaffirmed my faith in generations that came before me. He understood, and if he didn't really understand, he'd pretend to and try his hardest to help. He was just a mental health technician, but he cared about each kid on that unit as if he knew them from birth. He told me that his job wasn't to just make sure the unit was productive. He said he was there to save kids' lives, and boy, he saved mine. I was happy to be in an environment where people cared. My favorite nurses, Ms. Yvette and Ms. Lynn, both snuck me snacks when I didn't like the food the hospital served. I was in a facility where people cared and it made me forget about the fact that Emma's lies had gotten me there.

I wrote six chapters of the novel, about my experiences in the past year, while inside the hospital for my five-day stay. I wrote them on plain printer paper with bright orange marker. "Black American Psycho" by Ernest Baker, my favorite writer at the time, heavily influenced the novel. I wanted to save face and make sure the world knew I wasn't as villainous as Emma wanted the world to believe.

Mr. Marcus and Ms. Yvette treated me like their own child, and I could not get over it. I promised I'd send them a copy of the novel when I finished. Everyone there was so proud of me. I will go on the record and tell you that Mr. Marcus did save my life, and Ms. Yvette and Ms. Lynn also played substantial roles in helping me realize I'd get past what I'd gotten myself into. I am forever indebted to them.

I was released on Wednesday, August 19th. I got home and realized I'd received multiple letters while away. One was from a girl whom I'd recently developed a liking for before I went into the hospital. Her name was Dani.

Dani wrote to me and said:

Dear Lucas,
I know you are not okay. I know things
have gotten rough for you and I'm sorry
that I did not go through this with you.
You are a dream come true. You are the
Beacon that Trance spoke about. Do not
fall apart. Text me when you're out. I want
to make sure you know that I love you and
care. Don't let me down. Write like you
are running out of time.
Love, Dani.

I was happy to receive support from so
many people, but Dani's letter stuck out the
most. It was short and simple, much like her
at first glance, but it held a deep level of
emotion, also like her. She was, still is and
always will be an important human being for
whom I feel a deep level of admiration. I'll
never have anything but love for her.

My first text to Emma was:

"I'm out. How are you?"

I received no response. I went on
Instagram and saw that Emma had been out
partying the night that I was admitted into the
hospital. She went to a party and did drugs

while I was struggling to figure out a reason for breathing … because of her. Typical Emma.

I texted James Joshua to set up a schedule for gym time, only to realize I was blocked and unfollowed on all social media by James. Then I realized Emma was popping up in pictures with James. I put two and two together and began investigating. What I found out was very upsetting.

Emma Illiano slept with James Joshua while I, Lucas Sterling, was in the hospital due to her spiteful lies. James Joshua was 18 years of age. He statutorily raped Emma. He deserved to be in a jail cell for his actions.

I was hurt. Emma was out having sex with 18-year-old guys while I was in a hospital rotting because of the lies she threw on my name. I wanted to kill Tim Tylers and James Joshua. I also wanted to kill Emma.

I took a deep liking to Dani. The feeling was mutual so we began "talking." I wanted to be with her, but it was a mistake. Dani was an amazing, beautiful, thoughtful, innocent girl. I felt terrible for getting her involved in my life and my problems. She was so forthcoming with me. She genuinely cared.

Dani and I were cute together. All of Dani's friends loved me. I wrote her a really nice poem and recorded it and put it on my EP. I released it as a single. In it, I compared her to Calabasas, California. Everyone adored it.

I had three friends at this point in my life. Kyle, Juliet (Kyle's girlfriend, whom he'd been dating for a number of months), and Dani. Everyone else thought I was a lying, cheating, druggie. Emma was telling the world about me being raped, only she wasn't using the word rape. She was saying I cheated on her. This upset me because I knew I was a good, genuine person. I went to a football game and third wheeled with Kyle and Juliet. I never minded third wheeling because they were my best friends and their presence and relationship made me smile.

Emma showed up at the game. She sat down right in front of me and talked about me on her phone to everyone. She texted guys on the other side of the stands from Somberton (Emma's old school), whom we were playing, to come over and beat me up after the game. She had her friends, Kell and Kimberly, the people who I'd brought to the Trance concert, talk about me and taunt my relationship with Dani. I left the game early and walked home, crying a lot.

WHY'D THEY HAVE TO DESTROY ME, MOMMA?

I stopped smoking **cigarettes** that night after I smoked an entire pack on the way home. I ended things with Dani the next day. I'd decided I was going to kill myself in 2016 and I did not want to put Dani through that. She did not take the breakup well, and I did not blame her. She had very strong feelings for me and it essentially looked like I used her. I did not forget about Dani though … I remembered her every night before I went to bed. I hoped she would forgive me one day.

I knew I would definitely kill myself the minute I found out that James and Emma had had sex. I knew that nothing would stop me. I was going to release the novel and then kill myself after the world understood the method to my madness. I wanted my funeral to have a lot of **flowers and high heels**. I put together a playlist for the vigil that Drivestone would probably hold in honor of my death, like they'd done for previous students who died. I made explicit instructions that I wanted people to bring candles and I wanted them to dance when the music started. I didn't want to go out depressingly. I also didn't want people to think that my decision to kill myself was impulsive. I wrote 35 letters in the span of a week to all the people who I had words left to say to. I wrote what I was going to release as an open letter on Twitter to Tim and James:

Dear James and Tim,
I hope you know I killed myself because of your undeniable sexual cravings for girls who hadn't reached the age of consent.
I hope you are satisfied with murdering me.
With warm regards,
Lucas Sterling

I knew I had gone off the deep end once again. I was to finish the novel, have the character at the end kill himself, give out 100 free copies, and then kill myself, and let the world know that the narrative was my own. I wanted the world to know it was Emma's fault. I wanted to ruin her like she had ruined me.

Emma started texting me again after Dani and I split up and school started back. She wanted me to tell her that I was still in love with her. She wanted me to fall back apart. At the end of every call, her mascara would be running and I would wish I could step through the screen and wipe it away. I always wished her the best, because I knew what was to come for me.

My life became very depressing. Things began to fall apart. I thought that slicing my wrists to the white meat would cut Emma out of my life. I stopped listening to Trance. I stopped eating. I became a zombie and my parents hated watching me fall apart. I was in desperate need of a silver lining. I found it in the form of a **rose**.

Someone had been growing **tulips and roses** in my neighborhood, and I decided to take the **red roses** for myself. I took them, put them in a vase, and placed it on my windowsill. I'd decided that **flowers** were the motif for my life. I could never escape their scent. No matter what **flower** it was, it always reminded me of love. These **roses** symbolized something different though; they symbolized the rest of my life. **Roses** come, do beautiful things, and then leave. I was determined to do the same. My novel had to be the greatest, most inspiring tale ever, and it had to show that even the strongest don't make it out alive. I would not share details about my novel except with Kyle.

Emma called me on a night in early September.

"You're such a joke. I don't even care if you slit your wrists to be honest." She was drunk.

This night would have been our one-year anniversary. I'd told Emma earlier that day that I was actually planning on killing myself that day, but decided to move it back to the date I'd released my novel. Emma's response was not nice, as you can see. She cursed me out and said all I do is run. I cried a lot and considered killing myself right there, in that moment, but I then justified Emma's words with her intoxication. Even after we broke up, I always looked for excuses for Emma to be innocent. I did not realize that **sometimes things just fall apart** and there's nothing I can do to help those situations besides go with the flow. I had started to grasp the fact that things fall apart, but I still had hope that we'd fix ourselves.

"I'm going to introduce James to my family," Emma told me that night.

"Great, I'm happy for you. I hope he makes you happy because you deserve it," I said back.

I had learned that being happy for whatever Emma did always made her feel guiltier when she did things just to spite me. She didn't want me to be happy for her.

"I'm sorry," she said.

"For what? You're moving on, I'm happy for you," I said.

"Shut up. Everyone knows you want to die. I just don't want blood on my hands, so maybe we shouldn't talk anymore," Emma said.

It was astonishing to me that Emma could simply not care that the boy she dated for 11 months was going to kill himself.

Lilly Printo reached out to me, almost a year after our incident. I was hesitant but decided to talk to her and reconcile with what went wrong. We made up, and I let my guard down once again. I realized that it made no sense to hold a grudge when I'd be gone soon anyway. Lily became a supportive figure in my life. She had a boyfriend and she had genuine feelings for him. I was extremely happy for her. She had definitely learned a lot in the past year, and I saw so much in her. We didn't have any level of romantic connection; this made both of us all the more comfortable with each other.

"I honestly see myself marrying Charlie. He is so sweet and treats me like I have a lot more worth than I'd realized," she said one day.

I started crying at this statement. Everyone around me was with the person they loved and they were healthy and happy. I was all alone, crying myself to sleep with the image of James Joshua raping Emma in my head. I decided to get out of the house. I went for a walk and met up with some people from school. We grabbed some food and caught up on each other's lives. I avoided the question every time it was force fed to me.

"What happened with you and Emma?"

I wanted to respond with: "She ruined my entire life." But I always said, "Oh, the relationship was just not working, so we split up. I wish her nothing but the best." I always finished with a smile.

I did not want to be a nice guy anymore. I started trolling James Joshua on Instagram. I decided that I hated him. I wished that James would die. I wondered if Emma called him "daddy" when they had sex – I mean when he *statutorily raped* her. I wanted to know details. I was not jealous, but I'll admit I was curious.

I realized I needed to take a break from writing my novel to enjoy the little things in life before I ended it. I went to an amusement park by myself on a Saturday and then to see a movie by myself. I had a good time. I drank a lot of water that day and didn't eat any meat. Times like this knocked me back and made me realize that there's a genuine presence of purpose in my life.

I went to the same amusement park that I'd gone to with Emma several times while we were together. I rode all the rides we'd come to love. I cried in the bathroom once. I ate the same overpriced and over salted fries that we had eaten and sat at the same table we'd sat at the first time we'd came together. I wondered if she and James would ever go to an amusement park. I knew I had to stop thinking about James or I'd go crazy.

The movie I saw that night was a mediocre superhero movie at best. The soundtrack for it was killer, though. I began to realize how opinionated I really was. I always wanted to critique something.

Being honest, I really only went to the movie theater to conquer my fear of movie theaters. A friend in Chicago had been shot outside of one and killed two summers before and I'd hated them ever since. I was nervous that I'd see someone I didn't like at the theater, like James or Tim. I didn't, thank God. I knew if I ever saw one of them off of school property, I would fight them and get beat up because they were both strong, 18-year-olds who had friends who were also strong, 18-year-olds. I was a scrawny 15-year-old who could end you in any argument and steal your girlfriend with a single goodnight text. Checks and balances; that kept us all from hurting each other.

Life was weird. I had lost multiple friends. I had pushed some away due to them telling my personal business to Emma. For the most part, Emma was to blame for my lack of support. She had decided to tell every relevant person who cared about me that I was a druggie, delusional psycho, and they believed it because Emma was attractive. It's funny how guys will sell out their friendships for a *chance* at sleeping with someone.

Sunday was strange for me. Sunday had always been the coolest day of the week because I did literally anything I wanted. Emma used to call it my heathen day. On this particular Sunday, I wrote two poems and put them on Twitter, as the announcement of my novel. They were both snippets or scraps from my novel. I just tweeted the cover art, two poems, and the words "The Ultimatum of Lucas Sterling" and I blew right back up. I was back. I was better. I was regifted my fans and support. They knew what I wrote wasn't the drugs talking to me any longer.

I received my first opportunity to write for a legitimate journalism site the next day. I chose to write my first article about my friend, Playa Smit's, new album releasing that Friday. I knew this article had to set my entire voice in journalism, so I went all out. I did an interview with Playa and got an early listen to the album, titled "Hop Off the Balcony." I began working hard on writing the best article I could.

I had to finish the novel also and make sure it was released before the end of September. The reason it had to be released in September was because that is the month that Emma and I began dating, a year earlier. I was determined to save my name and gain revenge on everyone who'd wronged me.

I was having second thoughts about killing myself. I did not know if doing it would be worth it. I knew the article would probably attract other journalists and make me a key hitter for articles. I didn't know if Emma was quite worth my life. I hobbled around with these thought for a few days before I released the article.

SOPHOMORE

Knowing that this would be one of my last weeks of school, I was somber. I sat alone in the morning and wrote music. I had to finish my novel and release some music explaining the context behind my death, at all costs. Those two things are what kept me from killing myself and dying regular. My mom was proud of me and so was my father for working so hard on my novel. As Trance the Trapper had said himself many months before, "Blood relations are all that matter."

I had two college courses and two honors courses in my first semester of 10th grade. I was thankful that James and Tim had both graduated because I knew I'd probably have had a class with one of them because I was taking senior level courses. They were gone though, and that was all good. My teacher for the class I had with Emma posted the seating chart and had, of course, seated her right next to me. My luck. When I found this out on the first day, I panicked. I asked to go to the bathroom and then stayed in there until the tardy bell rang, then I went back to class. I walked in and discovered Emma Illiano in the flesh.

She was wearing an olive green dress and she looked her best. I stared at her. She stared back. Every time we made eye contact, things somehow hurt a little less. I realized Emma had a spell on me that day and every time she looked at me, I felt it. Even in a crowd of thousands, I'd be able to feel her eyes on me.

The class I enjoyed most, Psychology/Sociology Honors, had two of my friends in it. I had a fun time in there. The teacher, Mr. Matter, was very smart and could pull knowledge out of his brain like no other teacher I had seen. He was also funny, genuinely, and I related to his sense of humor. Mr. Matter knew me from my poem the year before at the competition. He was one of the teachers who came up to me and said nice things about my writing after the competition.

My next class was College Level English, with the same teacher I'd had for English 2 the year before. I was one of the only sophomores in that class, which was mostly filled with very bright, intelligent juniors. The teacher, Mrs. Sendlean, believed in me a lot. When I was flunking her English 2 class, she told me flat out that she knew I was smarter than my grades showed. I had never had a teacher tell me that before, so it stuck with me. The AP workload would be a lot, and I was very aware of that, but I was trying to be engaged. English was a subject I took seriously because it helped me learn a lot about writing.

Our lunch break came in the middle of English, so I was able to catch a break during what was probably my hardest class of the day, thankfully. I sat alone at lunch the first week. I wrote the entire time without even touching my lunch. Every day, the goal was to make the best novel possible.

After English, I had the class that everyone had warned me about: Civics and Economics Honors. I was interested in the subject and the information that came with it, but I was wary of the teacher. People said he gave massive workloads, so when I told people I was taking 2 college courses, I was referring to AP English 3 and Civics Honors. The teacher, Mr. Higgins, was actually a nice guy. He had a sarcastic sense of humor, which I was automatically a fan of. I came into the class with a bad attitude though, so you can probably imagine that I walked out with an even worse one. Higgins was a good teacher, and I learned a lot from him on the first day of the week. My brain had just been plagued with mean things said about him beforehand.

I wore all black on that first day and my hair hung down over my eyes. I was already frustrated with how things were going. On the car ride home from school, Kyle and Juliet got into an argument about food, so nobody was speaking when Kyle dropped me off at my house.

"Love you both," I said before going inside and recording a song I knew I'd never release.

I called Emma on the first night after school to talk.

"We can't hate each other now. We sit beside each other. We both deserve an equal education so let's end the problems. I'm over it," I said.

"I have a right to have a problem with you. You were a jerk to me," Emma said.

"I didn't send you to the hospital, go to a party and have sex with people while you were there," I snapped back. "I didn't get rid of all of your friends for you and then blame it on you being psychotic."

"You got rid of your own friends. You *are* psychotic and people only love you online. You're fucking crazy and everyone knows it. You are a lowlife druggie who doesn't deserve the opportunities he gets." Emma yelled at me.

"Just stop. Stop doing this to me. You make me want to die. Please stop," I began to plead as the tears came.

"Okay. Whatever," she said.

School only got worse. Emma brushed up against me every time she leaned over. She'd touch my hand. She stroked my leg when I started shaking. She triggered every edge of my anxiety. I couldn't speak. I sat across the cafeteria and watched Emma laugh and have a good time with her friends while I sat alone and wrote about how much I wanted to die.

Emma FaceTimed me often to ask for help with her math homework because she knew I was one of the best in our grade.

One day, we started talking about how weird it is to have a class together and Emma brought up the way I look at her.

"You give me the sexiest look on the planet. It makes me melt. You have to stop doing that," Emma says seriously

"Okay. I'm sorry," I responded.

Right when I was about to say goodnight, Emma took her shirt off and exposed her bare breasts on camera. She told me she missed me and that she needed me. We both got naked that night on camera and made mistakes. It didn't help the situation I was in. I regretted it and cried afterwards. It wasn't love and that hurt.

The next day at school, she started calling me baby. She'd called me that, along with other things, the night before on FaceTime, but I chose to pretend that did not happen. I was hurt. Everyone in school had ostracized me because of her but she still dragged me around on the low.

One day, one of Emma's really good friends, Kelsi, invited me to sit with her and a girl named Bailey. They both turned out to really like me and accept me for who I was.

"Listen, forget what Emma says. You are Lucas Sterling. You published a book and you're publishing another one. You saved kids' lives. Stop being so scared of a girl who will never in her life do the shit you've done at age 15," Kelsi said.

That statement made me feel whole again.

BE GOOD, DON'T DIE, DRINK WATER

It was a Saturday evening in early October that I met my ultimatum. Having finished my novel, perfecting it, and setting it up for a slated release on the 14th, I was ready to leave this world. I needed euphoria and I needed to signify that everything was being released from my body. I chose to go out by drowning myself in my neighborhood pool.

I had this plan in mind for weeks, so I had everything I needed. I'd been able to steal four of my father's 45 pound weights, and a chain from his shed while he was away on a business trip in the city. He wouldn't be back in town for another two days. I also was able to convince the man in my neighborhood in charge of the pool to let me sneak in and do some videos for a "film" I was making.

I wanted the world to watch me die, so I decided to livestream my demise through

Twitter. I had bought a waterproof iPhone case and a waterproof flashlight for it. I needed Emma to watch.

The weights I tied to myself had the names James Joshua and Tim Tylers written all over them in waterproof ink. I made it a point to show my audience this and to release my open letter to the both of them. I did not speak to my audience for the duration of the livestream; I talked through music and written words. It was almost midnight. I was ready to begin my show.

When I chained the weights to my legs and arms, everyone knew what was coming. I immediately received phone calls and texts, which I declined to answer. People didn't care about Lucas Sterling anymore or what he had to say. Only Emma's words counted. Before jumping in, I said my first words of the night, and my last words of my life.

"This is Emma Illiano's fault. Read the note I've published on this site." I held up a sheet of white paper with the URL of the site I had made to release all of my open letters and writings and my novel.

killlucassterling.us

The last thing I remember was my jump.

I am watching myself. They've laid me on a table and are trying to assess the situation. I imagine the table is cold. Not as cold as that water. I can't be dead. I'm still thinking. This is all I know. I don't think I'll make it out of here breathing, but if you would, listen.

They say that your life flashes before your eyes when you die and that's how I know that this is very much real. You and I just witnessed it all. You heard the narrative from the boy himself and I relived it once again and if I'd known how to do that before, maybe I would have never had to drown myself with the weight of what was once my entire world. Maybe I would have killed it then like I'm killing it now – this time without killing myself. Death, you were nothing but a dream for me and now I'm listening to you sing for me. I shower in your aftermath and too many times have I gotten caught on your edges as I watch you take the druggies, the successful, you take the happy, you've stolen the sad, and stripped us of our clothing and our protection. I watch you at the bus stop in my favorite city, plaguing the minds of the homeless who lust over you. You shot yourself in the foot so many times that it's hard for anyone to take you serious. I met my hero twice this year. I went Hollywood on my town this year. I met a lot of human beings that I'll never stop cherishing. I watched a woman whom I gave my everything to decide that I didn't have the basic human right to live a life of prosperity. I spoke to my idols and my name was plastered all over the world within minutes of a livestream of my death going up. I see my mother in the waiting room, waiting for your call. Begging for mercy. You can't even look her in the eyes without shame. This wasn't supposed to happen.

I
FELL
APART.

I don't know if I'll make it out of this room alive. I have come to terms with the wrongdoings in my life. But I will not let myself run out of time without publishing this to the world and clearing my good name. You and I just witnessed my life flash before my eyes. I'm not a bad person. I ruined my reputation as cute as the next kid. The difference is, I took my life seriously until I realized it was nothing but a joke to you. I catch all these glimpses of the emergency room. I think I see God somewhere; maybe this is his way of ungrounding me. My name is trending on Twitter. I catch a glimpse of Emma on her way to a party with her friends. They're watching the livestream closely. Emma can't believe it. She doesn't even cry. She smiles. I realize this and I realize I've got more to live for than to leave her, or anyone, satisfied. I decide that this is it. I have to come back. I have to finish my novel and I have to save face. I won't fall apart I won't fall apart I won't fall apart I won't fall apart

I

WON'T

GIVE

UP
COME ALONG COME ALONG COME
ALONG YOU CAN DO IT BREATHE
IN BREATHE OUT BREATHE IN
BREATHE OUT YOU CAN LIVE YOU
CAN PROSPER YOU CAN SUCCEED
COME ALONG COME ALONG
THOSE CIGARETTES HAVEN'T
CAUGHT UP TO YOU YET I KNOW
YOU GOT HER HIGH HEEL
CAUGHT ON YOUR SUIT PANTS
BUT WE CAN GET THAT FIXED JUST
STICK A FLOWER IN THE VASE AND
MAKE THIS REAL BREATHE IN

B R E A T H E   O U T

"WAKE UP, LUCAS!"

Suddenly:

"CLEAR"

BEEP

Lucas Sterling is alive.

ABOUT THE AUTHOR

Stephen Brown is alive.

AUTHOR'S NOTE / EPILOGUE

Lucas went on to walk out of that hospital with a messed up liver and a sliver of hope left. He is the everlasting embodiment of the adolescent struggle. Lucas would fall in love again. This time the feelings were healthy and reciprocated, with a girl who wanted nothing but happiness for him. She embodied every piece of the world that Lucas missed when he was stuck under Emma's witch's spell. Lucas may not have learned to be happy, but he learned how to cope. He learned to water his garden and let nobody step on his flowers. He finished, and published, a novel and he cleared his good name.

Lucas Sterling lived forever through the legacy of his words, his love for humanity no matter how against him it was, and through his characters.

I hope you find a little bit of him in you.

"LOVE YOU

BE GOOD

DON'T DIE"

- STEPHEN BROWN ♋

ACKNOWLEDGEMENTS

Thank you first and foremost to my family, including my loving mother and father and the coolest aunt in the world, Aunt Beck. Thank you to Maeve Gorman for the edits and outstanding support. Thank you to Elizabeth for being so utterly amazing, words cannot explain the beauty you put into this world. Thank you Ayo, GN, Addie, Patrick, Emery, and Isaiah for being the greatest people in this world to me. You changed my life for an eternity. Thank you to Cali and Julia for being my best friends. Thank you to Mr. Robinson. Thank you to Titus Gilner for being the first person to show me that I had a voice that deserved to be heard. Thank you to Connor Barkhouse and the rest of the gang from Philly. Thank you to Gilly. Thank you to everyone on Twitter who keeps my notifications on, I know that's a hard job, haha! Thank you, Ernest Baker, for inspiring me to write every single day and for inspiring this novel. You have been one of the most important human beings to enter my life, and I hope you don't ever leave. I am honored to call you my hero and my friend. Thank you to Sandwich Gang / Posse /

Tribe. Without you, this would be nothing. Thank you to Kyle Ennui and Kyle Mantha. Thank you to JITTA ON DA TRACK for doing the front cover art. You are a god.

Thank you to Lin-Manuel Miranda and Alexander Hamilton for making this a non-stop effort for me. Thank you to Parkwood High School. Thank you to my brother for being the first artistic person I ever met. Thank you to Chance the Rapper, for saving my life when I was ready to die, literally. Thank you to Dalia for changing my life and showing me love that I didn't always deserve. Thank you to Emma Camp. Thank you to Leandra and Nicole and Sofija. Thank you to everyone I meet up with after third block everyday. Thank you to Kylie. Thank you to my best friend and my rock, Cara. Thank you to Samantha.

WITHOUT YOU ALL, THIS NOVEL WOULD PROBABLY SUCK.

Made in the USA
Charleston, SC
07 November 2016